Face to Face Selling

The Art of Creative Confrontation

Arden Glen Press
Box 1131
Lisle, Illinois 60532

First printing 1985

Face to Face Selling

The Art of Creative Confrontation

by Bart Breighner

Arden Glen Press
Lisle, Illinois

iii

To Bill Keefe for invaluable editorial assistance

*To Alistair "Sandy" Campbell, whose creative contributions
helped make this a much better product*

To my wife Karen, my most constructive critic

Dedication

This book is dedicated to the great World Book organization. My thanks go particularly to the magnificent World Bookers with whom I was associated for 20 enjoyable years. Their enthusiasm and tireless work in the cause of better education has been an inspiration to me throughout my career. This book is the essence of that inspiration.

Who needs this book?

Yes, it's about selling. But it's not just for "salespeople". It's for anyone who can benefit from learning what I call "The Art of Creative Confrontation".

You want to Become More Persuasive?
If this is your goal, you will find that by absorbing the philosophy in this book, and by using the techniques discussed here, you will become a stronger, more effective person in all of your dealings with others.

You are New to Selling or You are Considering It
If you fit into this category, this book can be your "survival kit." It will help you to handle the setbacks that new salespeople face. It will give you an understanding of the Law of Averages. It will explain to you in simple terms the creative sales process that will enable you to turn prospects into "buyers" and have them be glad they bought!

You are an Experienced Salesperson and Your are Doing Great!
Tremendous! Then this book will help you stay on the roll you are on and give you the impetus you need to make even bigger things happen. You will see that you are doing a lot of things right and be reminded of some things that you need to begin doing again. It will trigger your brain into action to cash in on new opportunities that exist for you right now!

Does this Book Apply to Your Particular Situation?

Absolutely! Doctor, lawyer, merchant, chief...whatever you do, you can use the skills explained on the following pages. It makes no difference what type of work you do, or what type of selling you are involved in. The principles discussed in this book involve dealings with "people," not just products or services. It really doesn't matter whether you are selling in homes or businesses. It makes little difference whether you are demonstrating on a one-to-one basis or if you are dealing with groups of people in a "party-plan" atmosphere. Because there are so many common elements in the "people business" a high percentage of the ideas found in this book are certain to apply to you.

Much of what you do in your personal life is "selling" someone else on something — from a proposal of marriage to the choice of a restaurant or a movie. A lot of daily living comes down to persuading someone else to accept an idea or proposal that you believe in.

So whether you never knock on a door to sell Avon...work for one of the fine companies that use the Party Plan...or call someone up to see if you can get an appointment to sell an insurance policy...you'll find lots of good ideas in this book that you can use in other ways every day. And, of course, if you **do** choose a career in sales...well, I've had a very successful one, and I'm going to teach you everything **I** know about what it takes to succeed.

What is "Face to Face" Selling?
It Just Means that Someone is Getting Through to Someone Else

The expert waiter or waitress who serves your food with a flourish and makes you feel like you're their "best customer" is getting through to you. They're selling the merits of the restaurant itself...they're selling the quality of the food...they're sending you home with a full stomach and a warm, comfortable, "pampered" feeling that is sure to bring you back. By doing the job right, they are "pre-selling" an undetermined number of other meals that you will buy at the restaurant because you will want to come back for more.

The doctor who talks to you in a gentle, soothing, "fatherly" manner when you are in pain or upset about some annoying symptom is getting through to you. He is selling you confidence in his professional skill. He is selling you on the importance of following his advice carefully and diligently. He is selling you on the fact that what he does is worth the bill his secretary will hand you before you leave!

The auto mechanic explaining your car's problems...the sixth grader sweet-talking you into letting him mow your lawn so he can save money for summer camp...the preacher, the plumber, and the politician — they're all trying to get through to you. They are "selling you." And their selling skills are what determine their success or failure.

Face-to-Face Selling is the art of convincing, the use of learnable techniques to close a transaction, the application of basic rules or principles to show a prospect or customer that you have something he or she needs. It is **not** conning, not intimidating, and definitely not one-way communicating.

Table of Contents

Page

Chapter

Chapter 1

THE ART OF CREATIVE CONFRONTATION

I've been practicing what I call "The Art of Creative Confrontation" for over 20 years now. I've decided it's time to pass along some of the useful things I've learned to others.

When I sat down and really thought about it, I realized that the most important skill successful salespeople (and successful people in general) have is not the "gift of gab," or an engaging personality, or a winning smile. It's the ability to deal with others effectively through what I choose to call "creative confrontation." People who succeed in selling are almost always masters of this art. Yet, I know it isn't necessarily something you're born with. You can learn it!

Does "Confrontation" Sound a Little too Menacing?
Don't let my term "creative confrontation" give you the

1

wrong impression. Some people think a confrontation has to be an angry, hostile scene with a lot of yelling and screaming. It doesn't. Actually, I think most of the yelling and screaming people do is an attempt to avoid a confrontation with the truth — about themselves, or about some part of their lives that isn't working for them.

Facing Things Boldly

Webster defines the term "confront" as to "face things boldly." And that's exactly the way I mean it. In all my years in Face-to-Face Selling, the biggest winners I've known have been the ones who knew how to face things boldly. Not with anger and hostility, but with courage and determination. They came to grips with each situation they faced. That's what makes a confrontation "creative." And that's the only kind of confrontation I'm interested in.

Consider a case. I was selling advertising space. The prospective client, owner of a $10 million business, almost refused to come to the phone when I called him. Even when he did, he sounded hostile from the first word.

"I'm busy," he said, "very busy. No, I'm not really interested. You can stop by if you want but I can't guarantee I'll be here. Even if I am, I may be too busy to see you. Do what you want. But I warn you you're probably wasting your time."

When I got to his office, his secretaries — plural — were cagey but nice. "He's very busy," one of them told me, "but would you like a cup of coffee?" I would, and did.

After a few minutes, Mr. Hostility came out, looked me over and said, "I see you got coffee. Why didn't you order breakfast?"

"I didn't want to push my luck," I replied, thinking how much I'd really like to get up and walk out on this turkey (most inexperienced salespeople would have). But I was already applying The Art of Creative Confrontation. And I waited.

Finally, The Boss came out again, saw that I was still there and said roughly, "Okay, you've got about two minutes."

At this point, I sensed that I had already shown him I was not intimidated by his bluster. I had taken the right stance and he had invited me into his office.

To cut a long story short, twenty minutes later I had closed the sale and had an invitation to lunch. Yet, without the Art of Creative Confrontation, I might never have stepped into the prospect's office. By "facing things boldly" and taking the right stance, I did what I had come to do.

There's no doubt that the Art of Creative Confrontation works. Let's take a closer look and see how...

The Goal of Every Creative Confrontation

Your goal will vary with the nature of the confrontation. If you're in sales and what you're "facing boldly" is the prospect, your goal is the sale. Whether you're selling or not, the goal in any confrontation is always *to resolve the situation to your satisfaction.*

The 5 Rules of Creative Confrontation

To become a master of this most priceless art, be sure to practice each of these 5 rules very carefully:

1. *Maintain the right STANCE.*

2. *Keep your COOL.*
3. *Be PREPARED with facts.*
4. *Use your COMMON SENSE.*
5. *Let the other person keep his or her DIGNITY.*

Now, let's look at some examples...

THE FIRST CREATIVE CONFRONTATION YOU NEED TO HAVE IS WITH YOURSELF. Never forget that, "If you're not satisfied with your progress, the person responsible is always available for consultation." It's you. That face that stares back at you from the bathroom mirror each morning is the most important person in your life. And one of your most important lifelong tasks is to get to know that person — charm, talent, warts and all. The better you know that person, the better your chance of getting the kind of performance you want out of him. So face that bathroom mirror boldly.

YOUR SECOND CREATIVE CONFRONTATION IS WITH THE NEW DAY AHEAD. Every 24 hours, you get a new opportunity to "face things boldly." Shrink from it and another day is wasted. Apply the Art of Creative Confrontation and — this I promise — something good will happen.

Many people overlook the fact that each day breaks down, quite naturally into little pieces — each a creative confrontation opportunity itself. For the dentist, each piece is a patient. For the student, each piece is a class. Life just never stops giving us another chance — another opportunity to "face things boldly."

Ask yourself, What are the important pieces of my day? These are the confrontations that can lead you to success — if you use them *creatively to resolve each* situation to your satisfaction. And you can if you wish.

Learn Creative Confrontation and You Can Even Fire Someone and Still be Friends

I was on a flight from Pennsylvania to Chicago. The strapping young fellow in the seat next to me had been *dropped* from the Washington Redskins football team that very day and was on his way back home in the western part of the United States. Although he was really disappointed about not making the team, he couldn't say enough about the Redskins' organization and its coaches and management. Why? First, because he had a good experience during his time in camp, but maybe more importantly, how they "confronted" him about not making the team. He told me that the general manager assured him he had the talent to play in the NFL — he admired both his athletic ability and his attitude, but unfortunately he was caught in a situation where they simply had too many good athletes at his position.

The young athlete contrasted that treatment to a previous team that had given him a tryout. His feeling toward that team and its coaches was one of bitterness. The major difference was the quality of the *"Selling Job."* The additional expenditure on the part of the Redskins for the goodwill was probably 20 minutes of the general manager's time praticing the "Art of Creative Confrontation."

This reminds me of an experience I had some years ago when I was in charge of the World Book Sales Force. I had the rather unpleasant task of firing a highly paid sales manager. Even though I liked the guy and got along with him well on a personal level, his performance simply did not justify his cost to World Book. So I invited him into my office to tell him.

Now, the important thing in any situation like this is to remember those **5 Rules of Creative Confrontation.** First, the STANCE I took with him was friendly and respectful. Second, I kept my cool — there was no point, after all, in getting angry. Third, I was well PREPARED with facts that supported my decision. (Actually, I never had to use them. He knew.) Fourth, I used my COMMON SENSE in my whole discussion with the man — and appealed to his. Fifth, I never once questioned his innate talent and ability so I allowed him to retain his DIGNITY.

The interesting thing about this experience was that the man left our "exit interview" in good spirits, determined to move on to better things and without anger or bitterness toward myself or the World Book organization.

He was so jovial, in fact, that his boss asked me, "Are you sure he knows he's been fired?" This man, a "blood and guts" type, had assumed that the interview would be a "chewing out" with a lot of personal attack and defense, ending in bitterness and hostility. It didn't happen that way — it didn't have to — because I made a point of practicing The Art of Creative Confrontation.

So, you see, creative confrontation skills can be valuable to you in selling a product or equally beneficial to you in selling a person on accepting your way of thinking. The style you choose to use in "facing things boldly" should be tailored to the situation. Often, it means knowing

6

"how to step on someone's shoes and not mess up their shine."

Let's Look at the 5 Rules of Creative Confrontation in a Little More Detail

1. STANCE Although I'm not as cynical as the philosophy expressed in the bestselling book *Winning Through Intimidation,* I have to admit that I got a message from it that has had a strong impact on me: "The outcome of every personal encounter depends to a great extent on the psychological stance you bring to that encounter." If you feel less than equal to the other party, you have a problem.

One of the best real estate salesmen I know showed a parcel of land that was actually one segment of a large estate. The prospects seemed interested but thought the price was too high. The salesman responded by telling the prospects that four other similar pieces of land had sold at proportionate prices — and he pointed out why this property was in the same ball park: the type of house, picturesque, rural setting, and so on. Then he said he would be leaving town on Monday but that, if the prospects were still interested, they could call him at home over the weekend. At that point he stopped selling.

By telling him about his Monday departure, he had left them with two things: a) a sense of urgency that they had better make a decision and get to him before Monday; b) the feeling that it didn't matter to him that much if they bought the land or not — that it was well worth the price and he'd probably have another buyer waiting when he got back from his trip.

Needless to say, the prospects called Sunday night and

7

he got the sale. His *stance* had been exactly right.

2. COOL This is a matter of staying relaxed, no matter what happens. Your prospect will be more relaxed if you are. (We've all heard of the guy who doesn't have ulcers, but is a carrier.)

Suppose the prospect says, "No, I don't want any of the household items you're pushing. They don't go with my decor." You answer, calmly, "Quite right, they don't. I see you like modern furnishings. I'd like to show you our line of decorative pieces that would go beautifully with the way you've styled your home. I can get you practically anything you need."

In other words, *don't panic when you hear the word "no."* It's often more a challenge than a refusal. Stay cucumber-cool, positive, and helpful. *Never feel* you've been put down.

3. PREPARED In a later chapter, I want to go into detail about the importance of having a well-prepared sales talk. At this point, let me just say that everything you do will go better if you "do your homework" first.

If you're selling fine wines, know the region they come from, how long they have aged, the temperature they should be served at. A lot of the selling you do is guiding people through unfamiliar territory. Make sure you know the way yourself!

4. COMMON SENSE Some call it "traditional wisdom." It's my favorite way of avoiding the "booby traps" that every sales situation is strewn with.

What booby traps? Well, suppose you and the prospect find you have a mutual acquaintance — someone you don't care for very much. Resist the temptation to tell the prospect you think this other guy is a jerk. The prospect may consider him a good friend. Let your common sense make certain you keep your opinions to yourself.

5. DIGNITY I once knew a salesman who eventually turned to bus driving for a living. His problem was that he just couldn't resist trying to *insult* his prospects into buying his products. He'd say, "That other stuff you bought won't work. It may put you out of business."

In effect, he was telling his prospects they didn't know how to manage their own affairs. He kept chipping away at their dignity until they threw him out.

Starting no later than the moment you look into the bathroom mirror tomorrow morning, make each new encounter a creative confrontation. Face each one boldly and, this I promise, you'll be amazed at the results!

Chapter 2

TURNING STUMBLING BLOCKS INTO STEPPING STONES

Let's suppose you know your product. And you understand the basic principles of making your presentation. But something is holding you back. Maybe it's inertia, excuses, fear, imaginary problems. Maybe it's all of the above. But something is keeping you from getting where you want to go.

The problem is not uncommon — especially in people who are just starting a career in sales. In fact, I've often run into beginners who're all fired up with enthusiasm — and, six months later, they're out of the business. Trouble is, they're not sure why. Some mysterious "something" held them back — kept them from realizing all they had hoped for.

Well, fear not. I've run into a few of these mysterious

"somethings" myself. I call them "stumbling blocks." And, over the years, I've used The Art of Creative Confrontation to turn them into "stepping stones" to success.

Let's look at some of these stumbling blocks and see how you can stop *stumbling* over them and start *stepping* on them. Here's what seven of the worst sound like...

"I'm just not a born salesperson!"

"I don't have time to do it!"

"I don't know enough yet!"

"I don't want to have to sell to my friends!"

"I don't know who to call on!"

"I can't seem to get out my own door!"

"I'm no good at handling rejection!"

These are seven of the stumbling blocks I've seen many times over the years. Now, let's see how you can have a creative confrontation with any or all of them.

"I'm Just not a Born Salesperson!"

I don't know who it was who dreamed up the idea we're all born a certain way and can't change a thing about it. But they did a terrible disservice to humanity.

The truth is, salespeople are *made,* not born. That is an absolute indisputable FACT. I know it is. I've seen hundreds who could hardly get off the ground at first and later turned into fabulously successful people — the kind that new people, just entering the business, would describe as "a natural born salesperson!"

I know of one psychologist, responsible for selecting candidates for sales careers, who says that any "effective

12

person" can learn to sell. By "effective person," he meant anyone who had: a) a mature personality; b) some stick-to-it-iveness;" c) the ability to function in the world.

"I try to establish in interviews and tests whether the person is effective in a general way," he says. "If the answer is positive, and no other problems appear, the candidate stands a good chance." He doesn't say a word about any "magical gift."

Wondering: A Place to Start

Studies show more than half the population has wondered, at some time or another, if they could be successful in a selling career. *More than half!* And, chances are, there's a very good reason why so many people do so much wondering: *money.*

***

A Chapter 2 Thought

Half the failures in life arise from pulling in one's horse as he is leaping.

J.C. and A. W. Hare

***

Now there's no doubt that a successful career in selling can often mean big money in a relatively short time — even for someone without a college degree or any special social status to begin with. So wondering is a pretty good place to start. Just don't be one of the ones who do a little wondering, only to conclude, "Oh, no, not me. I'd never be able to do it!"

Don't Sell Yourself Short!

The worst kind of prejudice you can have is prejudice

13

against *yourself.* You don't have to be a "born salesperson" or a born anything. Give yourself an even break. Here's how...

1. *Remind yourself that doing a salesperson's job simply means bringing a product or service together with someone who is a prospect for it.* You take a product that *does* something for people. And you find someone who needs to have that something *done.* And then you show the prospect the product.

I don't mean to oversimplify. But that, in essence, is all selling really is. Keep that in mind.

2. *Remember that thousands have done it before you.* Most selling jobs have already been done successfully by others. You don't have to reinvent the wheel. "Buy the package" of the company you're selling for — their training programs, sales aids, pricing strategies, and so on — and put it to work. If others are making a success of it, so can you!

3. *Always remember "Rockbottom John!"* He was in his mid-thirties when I met him and it really did seem that he had hit rockbottom. He had lost his production control job at a nearby plant. Almost immediately after that, his wife, a registered nurse, lost her job. Worse, the strain of it all was getting to them both and the marriage was in trouble.

In desperation, John decided to take a crack at selling. He applied, was hired, and spent the first day with a manager who happened to be particularly good with sales beginners. The manager took the time to make several very effective presentations to show John how it was done. Then he said, "Now you try it." And John did.

The results were remarkable. Following the example of

14

the sales manager, John succeeded in closing his first sale. Little by little, a major change began to come over him. His worried, frazzled look gave way to a broad grin of pleasure as he realized that, for once in a long time, he was going to have a day when things went right for a change.

"Rockbottom John" never went back to production control. His income from selling soon topped his old job by far. His marital situation improved and, when he looked back on the day he lost his job at the plant, it seemed to him it had been his "lucky day." It had, after all, led him to a brand-new career!

"I Don't Have Time!"

A lot of people have said it: I need the money...I like the product...I like the way the company sells the product. If only I had *time*, I could be a big success!"

To which I reply with an old adage: "If you want something done, get a busy person to do it!" If you really want to do something, the time is always there.

How Much Time Do You Have for Anything, Anyway?

How much time does *anyone* have? Well, there are 24 hours in a day and 7 days in a week. Multiply 24 by 7 and you get 168 hours in a week. Let's suppose you work full time and you sleep about the same amount of time as most other people. Here's what it looks like...

Hours in a week *168*
Hours spent working *40*
Hours spent sleeping *56*
TOTAL TIME LEFT OVER *72*

So you've got 72 hours a week left after you take care

15

of the main essentials. Okay, life is full of obligations — to spouse, friends, church, hobbies, home. But, let's be honest, a good chunk of those 72 hours just dribbles away. Put just 10 percent of it to work for you in sales and you have the equivalent of a full working day each week in front of your prospects! That's just *one-tenth* of your free time.

Remember that Your Free Time Isn't Really "Free"

How much can you make in an hour? Twelve dollars? Twenty-five? Forty? A hundred? That's what it costs you for each hour spent slumped in front of the TV. Remember that.

And remember something else: old habits may *seem* to die hard, but actually it only takes about 30 days to grow a new one. So decide what "free" activity you can do without. And plan to use that time, every week for the next month, to get in a little selling. Try it and, a month from now, you'll feel a lot better about everything!

Two coffee breaks a day may cost you 30 minutes daily. That's 150 minutes a five-day week. Seventy-eight hundred minutes a year. One hundred thirty hours. *Three and one-half weeks a year.*

Did you know Herbert Hoover once wrote a book in 90 days? He did it entirely by scribbling while he rode a daily commuter train.

You know the secret? You "gotta wanna!" Wanting is everything.

"I Don't Know Enough Yet!"

I've heard it so many times: "I don't know enough about this business yet. I'm something of a perfectionist. When I do something, I want to do it well. As soon as I've

16

done all the studying I need to do, I'll go out and become a big success!"

Let me remind you of three things...

Everyone makes mistakes. Cardinal Cushing once said, "Nothing in the world would be accomplished if we waited until we could do it so well, we would never make a mistake!" Believe me, you *can* make mistakes and survive to tell the tale. I'm an old hand at that myself.

Action cures fear. Saying you don't know enough sometimes means you're just chicken. And the funny thing about being chicken is that you can overcome it, a lot of the time, if you'll just *do something*. I know. I've been chicken myself a couple of times.

The prospect knows even less than you do. Most prospects can't tell how ignorant you are because — when it comes to your product — they're even more ignorant than you.

Most prospects assume you know everything anyone needs to know about your product. If they ask something you can't answer, don't panic. Admit you don't know the answer, promise to get it, then go get it and bring it back. Turn your knowledge gap into a positive, sales-producing opportunity.

Who Cares if You Mess up?

So what? Most things in life simply aren't the big deals we think they are at the time.

One day, I went to watch my son play basketball. He did well, I thought, and his team won the game. Afterwards, I went along with the other parents to congratulate the victors. As I approached my son, however,

17

I noticed he had a crestfallen look on his face. "Oh, Dad," he groaned, "did you see that air ball? I can't believe I did that. What a klutz!"

I had absolutely no idea what he was talking about. Then he reminded me of a particular incident during the game. I had had no idea that what he was referring to was an "air ball" at all. I thought he had deliberately passed the ball to a teammate who had, in fact, scored immediately. I had assumed the whole play was deliberate and so, I'm sure, had everyone else.

To my son, his minor and meaningless blooper meant that he had appeared to blow the game. No one else even noticed.

"I Don't Want to Sell to My Friends"

Some salespeople — especially those new to the business — fear that friends will consider them high-pressure nuisances if they try to sell something. Let me tell you something: this particular stumbling block is the biggest stepping stone of all.

They Deserve to Know

Got a good product? Are you proud of it? Then your friends deserve to hear about it, don't they? After all, you're not trying to pass off some junk no one wants. If your friends really don't need it, they can say no. But what if they buy a similar product from someone else — then come to you later and say, "I really needed it but I didn't know I could get it from you. Why didn't you tell me?"

I often heard about this kind of thing happening when I was in charge of sales at World Book. New sales people would come to me, furious with themselves, and say, "I can't believe I was so dumb! My friend just bought that other encyclopedia — the one that's so much more expensive than World Book — and now they tell me they'd have preferred World Book if only they'd known I was selling it!"

The worst part of it is, a situation like this makes you look as though you're not proud of what you're doing. So your friends will hesitate to tell other friends because they think you're trying to hide it. So one lost sales opportunity may produce several other lost sales opportunities!

Every single person you know — even the "nodding acquaintances" — sits at the center of a circle of friends, relatives, co-workers and business associates; — any one of whom may be an excellent prospect for what you have to sell.

Practice Your Presentation with Friends

A great way to let friends in on what you're doing is to ask them to let you practice your sales talk on them. Ask them to be your "guinea pigs," then do the best job you can. You'll get some sales and, probably, some referrals, too. (This technique works especially well in party plan selling.) Make it seem as if your party is a "dry run." Then watch the orders pour in!

A New Career?

Practicing your presentation with friends, you may introduce one or more of them to a new career in sales. It's happened more often than you might think. In fact, your friends and relatives may include some great recruiting prospects and — since most companies reward you

19

handsomely for bringing in new sales recruits — you may reap a double benefit.

Enthusiasm is always infectious. And, if your product is good, you aren't imposing on anyone by telling them *how* good. And remember that even the best friend in the world probably won't buy something just because it's you that happens to be selling it — especially if it's a "big ticket" item! Even if it's a little ticket item, they aren't risking much if they buy *one.*

"I Don't Know Who to Call on!"

If you're applying good prospecting guidelines, you'll always have someone to call on. Yet — year in and year out — I've heard this complaint.

Prospecting is so important, I've devoted the whole of Chapter 5 to it. So we'll come to a lot of the details later. Meanwhile, let me tell you a couple of stories.

The Night Before and the Man Next Door

This story was told to me some years ago by a wonderfully successful salesperson. When he was just getting started in sales, he found himself lying awake one night, wondering if he was going to make it. He kept tossing and turning and worrying and fretting. Finally, his thrashing about woke his wife, who wanted to know what was keeping him so restless. He told her.

"Listen," she said, "get up right now and write down the name and address of the first person you're going to call on tomorrow morning. Then get some sleep so you'll be fresh and awake enough to make the call."

He followed her advice and, mercifully, drifted off to sleep. Next morning, he took the piece of paper he had left on the night table, called, and made an appointment.

Feeling better about everything, he drove across town to meet his prospect and ran into a disappointment. "I'm terribly sorry," said the receptionist, "but Mr. Smith was called away unexpectedly. He won't be back until tomorrow. He asked me to call you and re-schedule but you'd already left."

Looking very downcast, the salesman thanked the receptionist and turned to leave. Suddenly, she jumped up. "Hold on a minute," she said. "As long as you're here, maybe you ought to talk to the company next door. They ought to be interested in your product, too. Tell Marge, the receptionist, that I said I thought it might be a good idea if she could get her boss to talk to you for a minute or two!"

So next door he went. And Marge got him in to see Mr. Brown, her boss. And what do you think happened? He got the sale, plus three referrals that turned into customers that same day, plus a new appointment to see his original prospect the next day.

When he got home with that "good, tired feeling," that evening, the first thing he did was give his wife a big kiss and a hug for her moral support and her excellent idea. The second thing he did was take a piece of paper and write on it, "The night before and the man next door."

As this salesman finished his story, he opened his wallet and took out the piece of paper. It was kind of yellow and crumpled. But the words he had written on it years before summed up his whole philosophy of selling. And they had helped turn a sleepless night into a brilliantly successful career!

The moral of the story is that, although the hardest

21

door to get through is your own, it's a lot easier to get through it if you've got some place to go. Even if that doesn't work out, there's probably another opportunity as good or better right there.

The Swing and the Tricycle

I once knew a sales trainer who told me about one particular trainee he took out on the road one day. The trainee wanted to drive, drive, drive, it seemed and, after a call at a private home, he said to the trainer, "Let's go! I've got another prospect on the other side of town."

"Hold on a minute," said the trainer, "your market is families with young children, right?" "Right," said the trainee. "Well," said the trainer, "Look at that house next door. What do you see in the yard?"

The trainee looked. "Er, a swing set and a tricycle."

"Yes," said the trainer, "and, while it's possible the adults may occasionally use the swing set, there's not much chance they get a lot of use out of the tricycle. So what does that tell you?"

"Kids," said the trainee, "They must have kids."

"Right," said the trainer. "And that makes them prospects. So, before we go driving all across town, let's stop in next door and see what happens!" So they did. And made another sale.

"I Can't Seem to Get out my Own Door!"

It's true: "The hardest door to get through is your own." But, if you'll just grab yourself by the collar and *force* your way through it, all the other doors will be much easier! Isn't that nice to know, when you really think about it? It means you get rid of the hard part *first!*

At Least Put Your Hat on

One of the greatest salespeople I've ever met, Monica R., tells me that, when she gets up in the morning, the first thing she does is put her hat on. "I always feel a little silly," she says, "walking around with my hat on. And the sillier I feel, the more anxious I am to finish dressing, eat my breakfast and start my day! In fact, I just can't wait to get out of the house!"

Get to Work on Time

Salespeople usually don't punch timeclocks. You're your own boss. If you're good, you can make five or six times the money most clock-punchers make. But being good usually means getting to work on time — even if there *is* no clock to punch and no boss to check up on you and frown at his watch if you're late.

"I'm No Good at Handling Rejection"

I've heard it so often. "What if they say no?" "What if they're rude to me and tell me to go away!" "What if they tell me to stop bothering them?" "What if I tramp around to prospect after prospect and nobody buys a darn thing?" "I don't think I can stand feeling like a loser over and over again."

Of course, it's human to want to be accepted, not rejected. But hearing someone say, "No" doesn't make you a loser. Not at all. I promise you, I've heard that word many times myself. Often, it's just a phase you go through on your way to "Maybe" and, eventually, to "Yes."

Let me explain some important things I've learned about rejection.

It's Nothing Personal

When someone decides, very firmly, that he or she absolutely does not want to buy your product, it almost *never* means they're rejecting you personally. In fact, they may have quite enjoyed chatting with you. To some people, a friendly, enthusiastic salesperson can be a breath of fresh air in an otherwise boring day. They may even want your product quite badly. They may just be unable to afford it. The timing may be bad for them, financially. They may have other commitments or problems that force them to refuse your product, even though they may be sorely tempted. What I want you to understand is that, when someone says, "No thank you. It's not for me right now," that does not mean, "You are a terrible, obnoxious person and I want you out of my sight right now!" So don't take it that way.

Take a Tip from Pete Rose

As he closes in on the record for the most hits in baseball history, Pete Rose is also setting records for the most *atbats,* the most *outs,* and so on. On his way to the Baseball Hall of Fame, he is also *failing* more than anyone in the history of the game. But he doesn't get hysterical and beat himself with a club after every failure.

On your way to a lot of "Yes's," you may well set a world record for "No's." Consider yourself lucky and laugh all the way to the bank.

The Luxury of Being "Down"

I remember a World Book branch manager who was quite concerned about one of his salespeople. "Sam is so down, these days," he said, "I know he was hoping to be a branch manager himself by now and he's disappointed."

"Well," I said, "if he wants to be a branch manager, he can't afford the luxury of being down." The manager passed this comment along to Sam who had the good sense to think it over and perk up. Eventually, he got what he wanted.

A man I know, now president of a major company, recalled the early years of his career. At one point, he had wanted to quit his job and his boss had asked him why.

"I haven't been to college," he replied, "and I'm no good at public speaking."

"So what will changing jobs do for you?" asked the manager. "If you're no good at public speaking in this job, you'll be no good at public speaking in your next job. Why don't you stay here and work on your public speaking skills?" And he did.

Summary

In this chapter, I've tried to give you some concrete examples of The Art of Creative Confrontation in action: how you can use it to turn stumbling blocks into steppingstones. One of the most important things to remember is that most of these stumbling blocks are just human fears and frailties that you can overcome by changing your attitude.

We're *all* subject to human fears and frailties. Even people who seem to be on top of everything. Early in my career with World Book, I remember hearing Charlie Jones, author of *Life Is Tremendous,* as a guest speaker.

At one point, Charlie said, "We all think we're unique. We think we're the *only* ones who are worried about something. We're not. For example, right now I'm up here.

trying to make a good impression on Bart."

I was at a lower level of management at the time and Charlie Jones was a successful, well-known, and widely respected speaker. I had been trying to make a good impression on *him*, and it amazed me that he would even bother trying to impress *me!*

So don't worry. You're not alone. We all stumble. Just practice the Art of Creative Confrontation and turn all your stumbling blocks into steppingstones.

Chapter 3

GOAL SETTING
AND
THE 5 P's

I was serving as sales manager in World Book's Pennsylvania office. With every member of our sales team pushing hard, we enjoyed a fabulous week. We actually sold 800 sets of encylopedias in that one week!

I got a call from the sales manager in World Book's New York office. "Bart? How in heck did you guys do it? What's the secret?" "No secret," I replied, "We just set some goals and we met them."

"Goals?" he laughed. He just couldn't believe that the simple act of setting goals and working diligently to meet them could be the cause of our spectacular performance. He seemed to think I was hiding something I didn't want to share with him.

I wasn't. I had willingly shared the "secret" of our success. And I'll willingly share it with you now.

Two Things Goals Do for You

Set yourself some sensible, achievable goals and, this I promise, they'll help you in *at least* these two ways...

They supply you with a handy reminder of where you want to go. At any given moment, and especially if you feel you may be straying off track a little, they bring you back into focus.

They keep you up on how far you've traveled. Knowing how far you've come is a terrific inspiration for keeping on to where you want to go.

Ask Yourself These 3 Questions First

It's a good idea to set your goals down on paper. Before you do that, ask yourself these three questions...

Have you a strong emotional commitment to achieving your goals?

Even though you may very badly want to reach them, can you handle, in a mature fashion, the possibility that you may fall short of full achievement?

Are you prepared to invest the proper amount of activity to achieve your goals?

A Chapter 3 Thought

Far better it is to dare mighty things, to win glorious triumphs even though checkered by failure, than to rank with those poor souls who neither enjoy nor suffer much because they live in that grey twilight that knows neither victory nor defeat.

Teddy Roosevelt

Anchor Your Goals in Time

You can choose a very ambitious goal like seeking
fabulous financial success. Or you can seek some modest
result in your family or personal life. A goal is a goal. But
one thing they *all* have in common is that they must be *set
in time.* "Some day" just won't do. And neither will "as
soon as I can find the time."

Suppose your goal is to increase your income by
$500.00 a month. If each sale you make contributes $50.00
to your income, you will have to make 10 more sales, each
month, to achieve your goal. How are you going to do
this?

Airlines are pretty good at getting from point "A" to
point "B." And they generally do it with schedules. So
make yourself a schedule. Hour by hour, day by day, plot
out how you are going to achieve that goal of 10 more
sales a month. And remember that any goal can be
achieved if you move toward it, in small increments, one
step at a time. Henry Ford once said, "Nothing is
particularly difficult if divided into small parts." Divide
your time into small parts and make sure each part gets
you at least a little farther on toward your goal. A journey
of a thousand miles begins with a single step.

When the great French philosopher, Voltaire, lay on his
deathbed, a friend came to visit and asked, "If you could
have 24 more hours to live, how would you spend them?"
Voltaire replied: "One at a time."

Goals Help You Learn Faster

One of the most successful salespeople I know — she's
head of her own company today — confided a few things
she had learned about goal setting early in her

29

career. A fellow beginner had asked her, "Jo, how long are you going to give yourself to become a manager?"

The question stopped Jo in her tracks. She realized that she really hadn't given much thought to goals beyond making or exceeding next week's quota. She had no real goals for her *career*. That very evening, she sat down with a pencil and a notepad and worked out her career goals for the next several years. It was a real turning point in her life.

Today, Jo says, "Anyone can learn to sell. But you learn a lot faster when you start out with goals. Goals build your momentum more rapidly. And they help you push obstacles and setbacks out of the way as you go along."

Tie Your Goals to a Specific Amount of Activity

Let's go back to that example of adding $500.00 a month to your income. Most salespeople can translate a goal like that into specifics pretty easily. In some companies, for example, that increased income might come from three possible sources: personal sales, team sales, and recruiting new reps. You can get our your calculator and figure which combination of all three is most likely to get you the extra $500.00. Then, if team sales are worth 60 percent of your effort, make sure that's what they get. Check yourself and be sure that what you're doing is in line with what you hope to achieve.

Goals Give You a Better Attitude

Salespeople with goals and a strong commitment to achieving them always seem more positive than those who don't have goals. In a way, goals are very effective protection from negative influences.

I plan to talk a lot more about attitude later. For now, let me just quote a very successful salesperson whom I have known for many years: "Goals for me are like the rudder on a ship. They steer me. I haven't sailed aimlessly in this business since I started sitting down and doing my goal-setting homework."

Watch for Pitfalls

When *you* sit down to do *your* goal-setting homework, keep a weather eye out for these three pitfalls...

1. *Don't make your goals rigid and unrealistic.* When Jo's friend asked her how long she expected to take to make the manager's ranks, she might have said, "Oh, five or six months." For a sales beginner, that would have been unrealistic, to say the least. If Jo had also maintained a rigid attitude toward her unrealistic goal, she would have been on a collision course with her company and its management policies. Jo would have been in for a big letdown and, chances are, her career would have suffered. As it turned out, Jo didn't make that mistake. Don't you make it either.

2. *Don't make your goals too modest.* One company I know used a mailer to recruit new salespeople The mailer asked, "How much money do you want to make this summer?" and gave respondents the choice of circling either $1,000.00 or $2,000.00 or $3,000.00. As many as 60 percent of respondents circled $1,000.00. And you know what? By the end of the summer, most had done a lot better than that. Just imagine what might have happened if they'd set their sights a little higher!

Don't sell yourself short.

3. *Don't kill a perfectly good goal with inaction.* If "the road to hell is paved with good intentions," then, undoubtedly, the paving stones are held together with unfulfilled goals.

Of course, no one really *means* to leave their goals unmet. At the time they set them up, they fully intended to do everything possible to achieve the whole shebang. But then the procrastination begins. And the distractions pile up. And the goal just sits there, neglected, to gather dust.

I have no solution for inaction except action. It comes back, once again, to having a "creative confrontation" with yourself. Face your goal boldly as a challenge worth taking up. Then get on with the taking up. And do it now. *Right now.*

Don't Kid Yourself
If you reach a monthly goal in 10 days, it may make sense to revise yor goal upward. Likewise, if you can't seem to reach a monthly goal in three, you may be over-reaching.

But don't pull the wool over your own eyes. Level with yourself. Is it really the goal that needs adjusting? Or is it your way of going after it?

Plan a Whole Lifetime
Some wry genius has said, "Most of us spend more time planning a two-week vacation than we do planning our whole lives. We think we can control what happens in two weeks. But a whole lifetime is just too big a task to handle."

But if you can plan two weeks, you can most certainly plan a lifetime in two-week segments. Decide where you want to be five years from now, ten years from now. Then break it down into bitesize chunks you can handle easily.

Remember to Review
Earlier, I pointed out that goals help you check to see how far you've come and how much farther you have to go. But that can only happen if you review periodically. So, when you sit down to plan your goals, plan when you'll review them, too. And tie your periodic reviews to the calendar. No matter what else is happening, review *on schedule.* It's the best way to avoid nasty surprises.

The 5 P's: Prior Planning Prevents Poor Performance
Fix that phrase in your brain forever. I promise you, those are golden words. Memorize them and think about them often.

To be specific, here's how I recommend you plan each day...

1. *Write down everything you have to do today.* Put down all the possible sales calls you were thinking of making — plus any administrative chores you have to do and anything else you can think of. Do it quickly, before your day starts.

2. *Rank everything in order of importance.* Ask yourself, "Is this activity directly related to getting me business?" Then rank it accordingly.

3. *Get rid of the dead wood.* There are probably at least some items on your list that aren't going to contribute *anything* to your business. Get rid of them.

4. *Decide which items are "urgent" and which are simply "important."* Be honest. No fooling.

33

It's Called Prioritizing

Do all of the above and, in just a few minutes, you have organized your day. You have *maximized* your chances of coming home later in the day, feeling like a conquering hero.

What you've done is called prioritizing. And it isn't hard to do if you're willing to be honest, courageous, and purposeful. It actually *forces* you to do some things you probably would not do otherwise...

It forces you to cross out activities that deliver comfort and comradeship but no sales.

It forces you to eliminate prospects and calls that may take 75 percent of your time to produce 25 percent of your sales.

It forces you to do away with nonselling activities — especially "waiting" time, office routine, or needless detail work that may really be masking procrastination.

Prioritizing Gets Rid of "Time Killers"

Here are the five worst time killers I've ever run into. If they sound familiar, use prioritizing to help get rid of them.

1. *People who think your time is their time.* Too often, this makes your time worthless. Cross them off your list.

2. *The disease called "telephonitis."* It afflicts a lot of people today. Cure it by hanging up and getting out in front of your prospects.

3. *100 kinds of distractions.* From listening to the end of the eighth inning to stopping for a snack. Turn the radio off and drive to your appointment.

4. *Errand running.* You know you'll be passing Tillie's Tailor Shop. So you decide to stop and pick up your shirts. Do it Saturday.

34

5. *Not listening.* Which means you may have to backtrack later just to check out what it was that someone told you. Learn to listen, take notes and check the details.

Rate Your Time

"I picture it this way," one of the highest producing salespeople I've ever known said to me one day, "I have at least six kinds of working time. And I rank them in order of importance." Here's his list...

1. Time actually spent with a prospect.
2. Time spent doing things to get in front of prospect.
3. Time spent getting information about a prospect's life, preferences, family and circumstances.
4. Time spent getting the names of prospects.
5. Time spent traveling to see a prospect.
6. Time spent updating my records.

"All six kinds of time are important," he said. "But number one is the most important of all. And all the others are to help me spend as much time as possible on number one.' "

Use an Eggtimer

Earlier, I mentioned *Telephonitis* as a disease to avoid. You can avoid succumbing to Telephonitis if you keep an eggtimer on your desk. Before you make a call, jot down the things you need to discuss with the person you're calling. For example ...

Call Mary Jones — Invite to Wednesday meeting —
Mention exciting guest speaker — Offer ride —
Encourage her to bring a sale to meeting.

Then call Mary and, as soon as she answers, turn

over your eggtimer and limit your call to the three minutes you'll have until the salt runs to the bottom. You'll rarely need more time than that to do what you need to do.

Charting Your Time

Your local stationery store has a wide selection of desk diaries or daily journals you can use to chart your time day by day. It takes only a few minutes to do it each day. Yet, as time goes by, what you eventually have is a priceless record of what you did each day, what worked and didn't work, and much more. It's well worth those few minutes it takes to keep your charting current.

Rating your time and charting your time go hand in hand. If the time you spend in front of prospects is the most important time of all, your records should show you what percentage of your time is spent doing that. It may not be enough. But you may never know unless you keep track.

Some years ago, one company did a survey that showed low producers spent less than half of the amount of time in front of prospects than the high achievers spent. How much of your time do you spend in front of prospects? If you don't know, start keeping records.

On pages 38 and 39, I've offered a couple of charts you may want to use in planning and recording the time you spend. I've suggested the kinds of information I feel is important. You may want to modify these charts to suit your own particular situation. Feel free to do so. What's important is that the data you enter on these charts match your goals.

Summary

Prior planning really does prevent poor performance. When everything you do fits into a plan — one designed to achieve specific goals — you always have a better idea of where you are, how far you've come, and where you're going. Here's a handy checklist you can use to plan...

1. Have specific goals.
2. Put reasonable stretch in your goals.
3. Schedule enough activity (presentations, shows, etc.) to reach your goals.
4. Allow sufficient time to achieve them.
5. Keep good records.
6. Revise your goals when it seems appropriate.

Weekly Planning

For Fiscal Week # _____ From _____ To _____

GOALS		RESULTS	
Pers.	Org.	Pers.	Org.

Monday	Tuesday	Wednesday	Thursday	Friday	Saturday
					Sunday

Time Log: Record of Daily Activity

For: _____

6:00 a.m. _____	12::15 p.m._____
6:15 a.m. _____	12:30 p.m. _____
6:30 a.m. _____	12:45 p.m. _____
6:45 a.m. _____	1:00 p.m. _____
7:00 a.m. _____	1:15 p.m. _____
7:15 a.m. _____	1:30 p.m. _____
7:30 a.m. _____	1:45 p.m. _____
7:45 a.m. _____	2:00 p.m. _____
8:00 a.m. _____	2:15 p.m. _____
8:15 a.m. _____	2:30 p.m. _____
8:30 a.m. _____	2:45 p.m. _____
8:45 a.m. _____	3:00 p.m. _____
9:00 a.m. _____	3:15 p.m. _____
9:15 a.m. _____	3:30 p.m. _____
9:30 a.m. _____	3:45 p.m. _____
9:45 a.m. _____	4:00 p.m. _____
10:00 a.m. _____	4:15 p.m. _____
10:15 a.m. _____	4:30 p.m. _____
10:30 a.m. _____	4:45 p.m. _____
10:45 a.m. _____	5:00 p.m. _____
11:00 a.m. _____	5:15 p.m. _____
11:15 a.m. _____	5:30 p.m. _____
11:30 a.m. _____	5:45 p.m. _____
11:45 a.m. _____	6:00 p.m. _____
12:00 a.m. _____	Evening _____

39

Chapter 4

YOU ARE
THE MESSAGE

Okay, it's test time. I want to test you on how you feel about sales as a career. Take a minute or two to check your answers to this little quiz...

1. *Sales is one of the highest-paid occupations in the United States.*

True   **False**

2. *In sales, you get paid what you're worth. In salaried jobs, you paid what the worst employee at that level is worth.*

True   **False**

3. *As a salesperson, you're more secure in your work because what you do produces profit. Most other jobs produce cost.*

True   **False**

Did you check TRUE for each of these statements? If

41

you did, you're 100 percent right. And I want you to remember that. Because these three points should be the bedrock of your *conviction* about your chosen profession. Your career in selling deserves every ounce of conviction you can muster. And the more conviction you have, the more you will project to your prospects.

3 Kinds of Conviction

Conviction about yourself...conviction about your product...conviction about your company. You need them all.

At a reent sales convention, I ran into Natalie, a diminutive, 56-year-old salesperson with a remarkable record of success. I asked her to tell me her secret.

"I talk to 'em," says Natalie, "and I make darn sure they know that what I have to say is *important*. If the husband's attention starts to wander, I poke him in the chest. 'Now, you listen to me when I talk to you!' I tell him."

Well I won't recommend you go around poking people in the chest. You just might get a punch in the nose. Natalie's particular *style* may not work for you at all. She gets away with it, partly because it catches people by surprise and mostly because it demonstrates her *conviction*. She makes her prospects feel her message really *deserves* their attention. So they smile at her chest-poking and listen.

Don't Be a Wimp

Nothing kills conviction like being tentative about what you have to say. If you come on apologetically with a pardon-me-I'm-sorry-to-impose approach you may blow the whole sale before you even get started.

As a consultant, I've worked with salespeople who sell magazine advertising. Jack was a guy who had a new territory with lots of prospects. He ought to have been doing great but he wasn't. I made some calls with him to see what was happening.

The first thing I noticed was the way Jack prefaced every statement he made with some phrase like, "We're *hoping* to do this and that," or *"Eventually,* we'd like to do so and so."* He made it sound like none of these things stood much chance of ever coming to pass. So I bought him a cup of coffee and made the suggestion to Jack that he drop all the "maybe's" and "we hope to's." I told him to make it clear that the project was practically ready to go."

Jack listened and took my advice. Within a week, his results had improved dramatically.

Some years ago, a young man of my acquaintance was making sales calls on schools in the Prairie Provinces of Canada. The company he represented had had a lot of turnover in sales reps and he was the most recent to work this particular sales territory. When he introduced himself to one particularly crusty school superintendent — who was well aware of the turnover — the super remarked, with a tone of sarcasm, "Oh, so you're the fellow who's going to give it a try *this* year!"

"No," said the young man, very directly, "I'm the one who's going to *do it* this year!"

The crusty old superintendent was so taken aback, he invited the young man into his office and, needless to say, within a year, the new sales rep had accomplished what a long string of predecessors had failed to do. All it took was conviction.

Conviction Breeds Believability

A good part of the success of World Book as a product comes from its being so widely accepted among educators. All World Book salespeople have an ace in the hole, which I used myself on many occasions. Late in a presentation, I might say as a closing "hook," something like this: "Mrs. Jones, don't take my word for it. Simply ask six teachers what they consider to be the best family reference set available. I'm confident at least five — maybe all six — will answer, without a moment's hesitation, "World Book!"

When you can make a statement like that, it almost seems as though you are doing the customer a favor by selling them the product. That's the best kind of conviction and believability you can have.

Be Wholesomely Opportunistic

Calling at the home of what appeared to be an excellent prospect, I found that the husband was out. "I'd like to hear about your product," said the wife, "But my husband won't let me invite strangers into the house when he's not here!"

I glanced around. It was a bright, warm day and I saw a picnic table under a large, shady tree in the backyard. "Fine," I said, "then shall we sit over there at the picnic table?" She agreed and I got the sale.

Don't Let Your Conviction Run away with Itself

A longtime resident of a small town in Texas decided

to run for sheriff. He canvassed from house to house. Knocking on Mrs. Tompkins' door, he began to explain politely that he needed every vote he could get. But, before he could let go of a half-dozen words, Mrs. Tompkins interrupted him in a fury.

"Sam Beekins," she shrieked, "you've been chasin' women, drinkin' the town dry and avoidin' work for years! And you expect me to vote for a no-good like *you*? Get off my porch before I set my dogs on you!"

Back in his car, Sam pondered the incident for a moment or two, then wrote, beside Mrs. Tompkins' name, just one word.

"Doubtful."

Conviction is a wonderful thing. But don't ever let it make you lose touch with reality.

Back Your Conviction

Fran was a successful salesperson who suddenly found herself with a new manager. Some of her co-workers chafed at the unexpected management change. Not Fran.

"Give him a chance," she said, "he's got a tough job. Let him get used to it. Maybe we can all learn something from him."

In her mind, Fran simply "bought" the new manager, lock, stock, and barrel, and began looking for his strong points. She adopted some of his techniques for herself and found things that were valuable to her.

Perhaps most importantly of all, Fran projected her loyalty to her co-workers. And her enthusiasm was infectious. Largely beause of Fran's positive attitude from the beginning, the new sales manager settled in nicely and was a help to the entire office.

Build Your Own Enthusiasm

The easiest way I know is to start by asking yourself these four questions:

1. *These* **are** *quality products, aren't they?*
2. *People* **do need** *them — and are presently buying them — right?*
3. *The company's marketing plan offers me substantial* **rewards** *for the results I produce, doesn't it?*
4. *The company has a proven* **system** *that's getting results for others, and that I can use, too, don't they?*

By the time you've answered "Yes!" to all four questions, your enthusiasm should have perked up considerably. Try it.

How to Stay Enthusiastic

Part of my reason for writing this book was to help you to increase your enthusiasm. Today there is a wealth of material in books and on cassettes that you can use. Take advantage of it. And one thing more...

Cultivate "Rainy Day People"

A friend came to visit me in Chicago. We played tennis at my club, showered, then went to dress. Opening his locker, my friend found that the cash in his wallet had been stolen.

He looked a little crestfallen at first but, as we drove home, he said, "You know, it's a darn good thing they only took the cash. I have about six credit cards in there they didn't even touch." A mile later, he said, "You know, I normally carry a couple of hundred bucks around. It's a lucky break that I only had $50.00 in my wallet." Then, as we were pulling into the driveway, he turned to me

46

excitedly. "Hey," he said, "I just thought of something. This is a business trip. Any expense I incur is tax-deductible. I'm sure my accountant will let me write off that $50.00 as a business loss!"

In the three miles between the tennis club and my home, my friend managed to convince both of us that having his money stolen from his wallet was the best thing that ever happened to him!

My friend is a very good example of a "rainy day person." He's a positive thinker and, whenever I need a boost, he's usually one of the first people I think of calling. You probably know some "rainy day people," too. Cultivate them. Their friendship is priceless. Here's another example...

I know a Cajun lady who began selling reference books for the first time when she was in her mid-fifties. A superb salesperson and a good manager, she also did an exceptional job of raising five fine children: a homemaker, an Air Force colonel, a Catholic priest, a banker, and a doctor. The doctor struck oil on some land he owned and became extremely wealthy overnight. He went to his mother and said, "Mom, you're 66. You don't have to go around selling books any more. I have all the money anyone could ever want. Quit this business and take it easy."

The Cajun lady turned to her son and said, "Boy, this business gives me something all your money can't buy. And I intend to keep on doing it!"

Her *enthusiasm* for what she did made it more important for her to keep going than to take an easy retirement at her son's expense.

Don't Be a Message of Bad News
You *are* the message. But don't let it work against you.

47

It happened to me once. I had been selling World Book without any service charge. Then the company changed the policy and introduced a service charge of one-half of one percent per month. In dollars and cents, it didn't amount to much extra for the prospect to pay each month. But it bothered me to have to tell them about it.

On my first day after I heard about the service charge, I made two sales. Within a couple of days, both had cancelled. I thought about it and realized I was the problem. I'd let this new service charge bother me so much, I was flashing a negative message at the prospect without fully realizing it. I forced myself to clear my head and concentrate on how inconsequential this service charge really was. Soon, things were back to normal.

The point is that it's really the *inner* you that's the message. And it's what goes on inside your head that counts most of all. Just the same, the *external* you is what expresses that message and it's important to pay attention to the way you *talk,* the way you *look,* and the way you *act.*

The Way You Talk

The way you talk is as personal as your fingerprint. As long as you have an acceptable level of skill in the use of words — and a reasonably pleasant delivery — you'll most likely do just fine. Don't worry about personal idiosyncrasies like a regional or foreign accent. Many prospects may find it "charming."

Telling corny or off-color jokes may offend some and invite rejection. Tell the truth, listen carefully, and don't argue or criticize. And remember that eye contact with your prospect as you speak shows confidence and increases

rapport.
  Finally, know when to *stop* talking.

The Way You Look

All of us have personal preferences in dress. A good salesperson, however, should save his favorite sweater and denims for weekend lounging around the house. We need to fit the norms of good business dress. I recommend you read Malloy's *Dress for Success*. You may find it a little more conservative than you'd like, but it's a good place to begin.
  Top salesperson Kay McGinnis says, "I need to feel good, outside and inside, so that I feel both prepared for the selling process and happy to be going about it."

The Way You Act

Walk in. Shake hands. Take your coat off. Sit down. Reach into your briefcase. Spread out the sales materials. Fold papers. Make a note. All of these actions express your inner message in some way — whether you want them to or not. Some call it "body language." Be aware of it and remember that what it *should* be communicating is enthusiasm and conviction.
  Another kind of action is *manners*. Remember that manners boil down to expressing courtesy and showing consideration for the feelings of others. *Care* about your prospect's feelings and it will show.

Summary

You are the message. You can make that message a compelling one through conviction and enthusiasm. And you can express it most powerfully through careful attention to the way you talk, the way you look and the way you act.

I'm ending this chapter with a checklist of do's and don't's that may help.

A Checklist of Do's and Don't's That Refer to Externals

Jog your memory. Run through the following list and classify each as a "Do" or a "Don't." Each item touches on some aspect of the externals that project what you are: that make you the message.

		Do	Don't
1.	Break in when others are talking		
2.	Smile continually		
3.	Sidestep questions		
4.	Tell the truth always		
5.	Chew gum while with a prospect		
6.	Give snap answers		
7.	Practice eye-to-eye contact		
8.	Listen when another talks		
9.	Wear socks that don't match		
10.	Brag about the kids		
11.	List personal preferences in food		
12.	Listen to myself		
13.	Talk incessantly		
14.	Spread rumors		
15.	Break a confidence		
16.	Criticize by name		
17.	Arrive late		
18.	Use first names		
19.	Crack off-hue jokes		
20.	Ask personal questions		
21.	Overstay normal welcome		
22.	Lose my temper		
23.	Need a haircut or new hairdo		

Chapter 5

PROSPECTING AND THE LIBK RULE

There are seven steps to successful selling and I'd like to start by arranging them in pyramid form. Here they are...

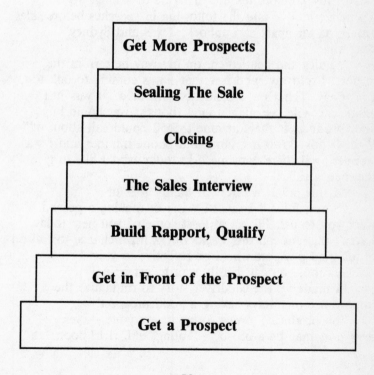

Prospecting helps turn the dream of success into the reality of money in the bank. I've carefully observed some of the world's best salespeople over the past 20 years. Some had great personalities. Some had okay personalities. Some had almost no personalities. They all had different physical attributes. But they had one thing in common: they all knew how to get a prospect and how to get in front of that prospect.

Always Have a Good Prospect

In my opinion, it's the first rule of selling. To dramatize it, I've said the following in speeches before sales groups as far apart as Lubbock, Texas and Sydney, Australia...

"Ladies and gentlemen, on my way here from the airport, I told my cabdriver that I was coming to talk to you today. "That's a coincidence," he said, "I was just telling my wife last night that I thought we should buy your product. Is there anyone there I could call about it?" Well, I took down his name and phone number and I was wondering if there's anyone here today who'd like to give the man a call."

At this point, a forest of hands goes up.

"Sorry, folks," I say, "I was just making a point I want you to use. I'll bet at least some of you here today haven't made a call this week. But, with a chance to call on a qualified prospect who'll be receptive to your presentation, you can hardly wait to get going!"

"I made up the cabdriver story to dramatize the importance of always having a good prospect!"

Top producers always know it; everyone — yes, *everyone*, may be a prospect. Young, old, rich, poor, fat, thin, whatever. Granted some are more *likely* to buy than others. But assume they're *all* prospects going in — then rate them according to likelihood.

A recent study shows 60 percent of salespeople *fail* to ask for a referral at the end of a demonstration. I have to confess, that makes me shudder. It means six out of ten are overlooking the most basic of all prospecting techniques.

A Tale of Two Stockbrokers

Here's a real-life example of two actual salespeople. The young guy is with a firm that strongly emphasizes grassroots prospecting. The other firm spends a full year training sales people on knowledge of the *product* — but is very weak on selling skills, including prospecting.

A Tale of Two Stockbrokers		
	Broker A	**Broker B**
Age	48	24
Sales Experience	15 years	none
Local Influence	lots	none; just moved
Training in brokerage business	full year; with salary	limited; on the job
Commissions earned first year on job	$22,000	$50,000

Does it pay to go out after clients? To be a resourceful prospector? The above is living proof that it does. Imagine...a man in his early twenties making more than *twice* as much as an older, more experienced man in the same business.

55

Prospects are Everywhere

Where do you start looking for prospects? At home. In the house next door. In the apartment across the street.

Where do you stop looking? At that point where the cost in time, compared to the possible gain, becomes prohibitive.

A professional salesman I know regularly questions his children about their friends. He gets a lot of information about those friends, their parents, their lifestyles. He is personally interested, but he is also measuring, scrutinizing, looking for prospects. Using that technique, he has increased his business tremendously.

From People to Prospects

In discussing prospecting, the art of finding potential customers, we are not talking about direct mail or direct marketing or classified or display ads. Those methods have worked for thousands of companies. Some firms have used them in combination with Face-to-Face Selling.

We are more explicitly dissecting a process in which the Face-to-Face person remains always aware that every individual may be a prospect. As a salesperson, you can school yourself to think of everyone in this way. People become prospects. You do not disregard their essential humanity. You merely accept the fact that each may represent a future sale.

As a major plus, you also start to see groups of persons as individuals. You can visualize each as a human entity with tastes, preferences, personalities, needs.

Each becomes a bank teller, a truck driver, a champion bowler, a beautician, a mystery-writer — and a prospect.

The Basic Technique

Like everything else in Face-to-Face Selling, prospecting requires technique. As always, technique makes your work more effective.

Descriptions of some tried and true techniques follow. If they spur some creative thinking, some exploration of still other methods, so much the better. *You can develop skill in the use of existing techniques and new techniques — or variations of your own.*

The key prospeting methods can be examined under seven headings.

● **Cold Calls.** The cold call is just that. You knock on a door or ring a bell and find yourself addressing a stranger who did not expect you.

Many Face-to-Face Sellers avoid the cold call approach as they would a nuclear waste dump. Others do very well using this method. If it's your bag, you can succeed in a big way. The essential qualities of dedication and perseverance come into play just as in other forms of prospecting and selling.

● **Personal Sphere of Influence.** How many persons do you know? How many are nodding, waving, good-morning greeting, and chitchatting acquaintances? How many rank as card-carrying friends? How many are in your neighborhood association, racquetball opponents, fellow churchgoers?

Think of this, in his Sphere of Influence Rule 250, champion car salesman Joe Girard states that the average person you meet knows at least 250 other people who might be prospects for your product or service.

If you think of it, you probably stand in some kind of social relationship to more than 250 people. You may have the beginnings of a great selling career in that group alone. Each of them has at least 250 friends or acquaintances who might be top prospects.

Why not start asking?

● **Referrals.** This subject has come up before. Most sales persons regard it as the closest approximation to the ideal prospecting technique.

It involves this: after making a presentation, whether a sale has resulted or not, the sales person obtains the name or names of others known to the prospect or customer. Others who may be interested in the product or service. Is it any wonder that this method has been called "The endless Chain System?"

Used correctly, it keeps you supplied with a never-ending list of potential customers.

● **Existing Customers.** Old customers, and especially *satisfied* old customers, can be prolific sources of prospects. Many will help you out of a sense of gratitude, or of belonging to the same club...your club.

My advice: never neglect those people you've already sold. If you do, you may find yourself in the position of the sales person who had no time for former prospects. This person repeatedly ran across old customers who had recently bought more of his products from other salespeople.

I've started many a great selling day by taking a few minutes to call on an old customer. I usually got a lead or two, and they always made me feel good about my product.

● **The Nest System.** You find Prospect Mary through a referral from a friend of hers. It turns out that she works in an office with a very close-knit staff. Mary refers you to half a dozen of these office friends. You have located a nest.

A "nest" may work, play, associate informally, or pray together. It may number in the dozens. For you it can represent a rich lode of prospects to be mined. One physician can refer you to 10 or 20 others who may be prospects. A man or woman working in a department in a manufacturing plant may do the same.

Most people belong to a nest of one kind or another. Why not make prospects of the members?

● **Centers of Influence.** Centers of influence differ from nests in one key respect: they consist of groups large or small of which you learn through an important person.

Examples? A plant manager refers you to his entire foreman staff. The president of a professional group gives you the names of all 22 members. A minister lists some of the more important members of his congregation.

Influence can also derive from wealth. A civic leader may have immense influence. So may a person who has won fame for some accomplishment.

The principle is simple. In following up on leads from a person of influence you are going armed, in effect, with a recommendation from someone the prospect respects.

The Buddy System

This happened to me. Early in my career, I decided to try working with a close friend, a former teacher and high school coach, who lacked selling confidence but "knew everybody in town."

Wherever we went, someone in the household would say, "Hi, Coach Mack." Selling became easy. I made the presentations; Coach Mack found the prospects. The combination of our talents and contacts produced a fabulous summer.

The buddy system has worked well under diverse circumstances and widely scattered communities. In one case the professional sales person's buddy had won local fame as a war hero. In another, the buddy was a person who had led a successful fight for civic reform. A third had gained fame on the basketball court only a few years earlier.

Varying Basic Techniques
I've mentioned variations on these basic methods.

They exist in quantity. Every top Face-to-Face producer I've known had some unique twists.

All were in good taste. All brought sales results.

Just for Starters...
For starters, think of the following possibilities. I have used them at one time or another.

● Calling on a prospect and finding no one at home, you leave a door hanger on the knob. It reads: "Sorry I missed you. Can you call me?"

● In a similar situation, you leave some materials for the customer to peruse. "Thought about another purchase?" the note on the materials reads. "Can I stop by Saturday?"

Hello. Sorry I missed you today. As your local representative, I can save you money and get you installed this week in an "easy trial offer." You sign no contract. Invite me to drop by, and in 10 minutes I'll explain the details. Absolutely no obligation. Call me today. Phone _____ or

● To obtain a referral, promise a reward. A thoughtful, ingenious salesperson working for a pay TV service used this technique repeatedly. Faced once with a prospect who showed no inclination to buy, the salesperson asked her if she could provide the names and addresses of others who bought the service.

To the salesman's surprise, the prospect went to the phone and started calling her friends and neighbors. Within 20 mintues she had four new prospects who were already half sold. And the lady had convinced herself in the process. She came back and signed up.

How many variations can you devise? Remember, the field in which you work will influence your choices.

Some Refinements

At least four of the prospecting techniques that I've noted involve referrals. The four are the straight Referral, the Old Customer, the Nest System, and the Centers of Influence methods.

You can obviously approach prospecting by any of the referral approahes on a long-term basis. Properly nurtured, a center of influence an supply you with the names of good prospects for months or years. The same might be said of the nest contact.

Just as obviously, you need both skill and determination to ask for referrals. You don't want to appear to be asking for too much. You fear a negative reaction. You have another call to make, and are in a hurry.

Forget the distractions. Get the referrals. Refine your technique through application of some or all of these refinements...

● **Have a prospecting goal** — or goals. Know how many centers of influence you want to develop in a given period — and find them!

● **Improve your memory.** Few things impress a prospect or client more than quick, easy recall of the name of someone of local repute who bought your product or service. Memory will serve you in dozens of other ways.

● **Get lots of information** — as much as possible. The prospect's job, family status, interests — they can all be important. Thousands of salespersons make calls after taking a name off a mailbox — or something else. In one case that took place in Canada, the salesperson, who was new in the area, saw a milk can with the letters NADP on it. He went to the door and, when it opened, said, "Mrs. NADP?"

"NADP? Oh. NADP stands for Northern Alberta Dairy Products."

● **Keep referrals and leads systematically.** A 3x5 inch card file served me well for years. Others have used other systems. But all salespeople keeping such records wrote down everything they could learn about the prospect. If the customer hesitates over a name, ask him to give it to you even if it looks like a cold lead. Then, with the customer's help, try to rate the prospect.

● **Rate your prospects.** Remember that you'll want to rate all the prospects in your file. The rating notation belongs on the prospect's file card.

● **Get to the new prospects while they are hot!** If you receive a likely looking name on Tuesday, you should be following up within days, not months. Two weeks may be too long. Use your desk calendar as a tickler if no other system works. You have, of course, to use common sense to get to the prospect at the right time.

The LIBK Rule
Can you pronounce LIBK? It stands for Let It Be Known.

It means that you can't hide your selling light under a bushel if you're going to make it in this demanding field.

Let it be known that you're in Face-to-Face Selling...and in what part of it. Whether you are selling brushes or houses, or enthusiastically selling Mary Kay Cosmetics, or cookware, paintings, or computers, prospects are everywhere. Virtually every human contact you make offers you an opportunity to Let It Be Known what business you're in.

That applies when you're traveling in an airplane. Attending a wedding reception. Chatting with someone in the line at the supermarket.

How do most people work into conversations? They find out "what you do." If you show you're proud of your work, and can make a good impression as a person, you may just find yourself with a brand-new prospect. One you didn't know you were going to get.

You can be selling all the time — even when you're not actually working. Selling yourself, observing, inventing methods, making notes — it all contributes, at all waking times, to your success.

Don't Overlook the Obvious
Prospecting calls, clearly, for application of one Sherlock Holmes principle: don't overlook the obvious.

While trying to sell some real estate through a brokerage firm, I had the validity of this principle brought

63

home forcefully. The real estate, a farm, had been on the market for two years. No dice. When the listing expired, I decided to take a shot at selling it myself.

I had subdivided the lot into seven different parcels. The first thing I did was call on the half dozen or so property owners whose land abutted on mine. I called them from Chicago, then visited them at their homes in Pennsylvania. Within three days, I had sold pieces of the property to four different individuals.

I'm not knocking real estate people. Many of them are highly skilled salespersons. But the brokers who had my listing had their eyes focused on potential out-of-town buyers. They had overlooked the obvious: that many land-owners may be interested in purchasing adjacent or nearby property.

Tools and Ratings

Now think tools. What others — besides your desk calendar and prospect file — will help you?

Your company undoubtedly helps. Does it supply lists? Door hangers? Gift pens? Company brochures? Anything that will simplify the task of finding prospects?

Are you using your car and its maps to the best advantage? The car can get you to presentations or calls — and thus to prospecting — or it can trap you. On too-long trips it gives you the feeling that you're working when you're not. Maps, used properly, save you time.

Some salespersons have used Polaroid cameras in prospecting. One office furniture salesman took photos at construction sites, then presented the pictures to the construction supervisor. Using the good will thus generated, he obtained the name and phone number of the person who would be responsible for furnishing the building.

That afternoon he would make an appointment to see the buyer.

Ratings? The best system seems to include A, B, and C categories. A represents excellent — a good prospect. B indicates a medium-good prospect. C identifie a mediocre one.

Some successful salespeople use a four-part rating system. Or a five-part one. You will want to use the system that you're most comfortable with.

Service What You Sell

Do you know how many people out there are thoroughly sick of poor service or no service at all? Some of them wear out telephones trying to get help.

Do you know how good you look if you take the trouble to show you care?

This doesn't apply to everyone in sales. But it applies to many of us. And I'm not suggesting that you follow through with service to prove how noble you are. Such follow-through has the purpose, rather, of *paying off* in one way or another.

Make a service call on a customer soon after closing the sale. Make sure the customer understands the product or service and is getting maximum benefit from it. Answer any question that may surface.

Then prospect. Obtain repeat business, then or later. Ask for prospects' names that may have been forgotten or overlooked earlier.

Do it quickly. The customer is usually most enthusiastic shortly after the sale and delivery. Cash in on this enthusiasm.

How to Use a Prospecting Card

1. How to Ask

After your demonstration, say to the Customer,

"I want to leave my name and phone number in a place where you keep your best friends' names and numbers — under the letters XYZ for the initials of our widget company, for example.

"Mrs. Customer, my job is to explain our product to three interested people a day. Who among your friends and acquaintances would benefit most from learning about this product? (Reach for the prospecting card and write down the referral's name.) Thank you! Who else? Mrs. Customer, can you think of one more? Thank you!"

"If you were in my place, which of these persons would you go and see first?"

"If your friends were sitting here in your dining room, I'm sure you would introduce them to me. Your friends don't know me but they are entitled to know what is available for their (family, home, etc.), so we offer this introduction card. My name goes here...yours goes here. Thank you." (Now fill out the rest of the prospecting card.)

Your goal should be to average at least two new referrals per presentation, whether you sell or not, with at least one signed introduction.

2. Door Approach with a Signed Introduction Card.

"Hi! Are you Mrs. _____? I'm _____. I'm so glad you're home! I was visiting your friend _____, giving her a presentation of our (product), and she suggested that I stop by and see you while I was in the area. This should only take about 12 minutes.

"May I step in?" What's it about? (Product.) Here's a note (fold and tear off the signed introduction card) concerning my visit. Is there a place where we can sit and talk for 12 minutes? Thank You."

Twelve minutes should cover rapport building, qualifying, and part of presentation, including need building and introdution of your product.

NAME			PHONE		
ADDRESS					
CITY					
BEST DAY AND TIME TO VISIT:					
WORK					
POSITION					
RECOMMENDED BY:					
CHILDREN	SCHOOL	AGE	SCHOOL INTERESTS		HOBBIES
PARENTS' INTERESTS					
Fill this out as you get your prospect info. Then after you have gotten as many as possible—ask person to introduce you by signing it			COMMENTS		

WHO HAS AN IMPORTANT SERVICE FOR FAMILIES THAT I THOUGHT YOU WOULD APPRECIATE HAVING THE OPPOR-TUNITY TO EVALUATE

THIS WILL INTRODUCE YOU TO

PLEASE LISTEN

SIGNED

Hints for Successful Prospecting

1. **Sell those who sell you:**
   - Insurance (Life/Home/Health/Car)
   - Dry Cleaners Services
   - Grocer
   - Banking Services
   - Clothing
   - Cosmetics
   - Legal Services
   - Dental Care
   - Tennis/Golf Lessons
   - Gasoline/Tires

2. **Remind yourself of prospects from your Xmas card address list**
3. **Review your High School Year Book**
4. **Sell business associates and former associates**
5. **See owners of your product or service**
6. **Friends from Church**
7. **Parents of childrens' friends**
8. **P.T.A./Garden Club/Little League or other groups with whom you have involvement**

Chapter 6

GETTING IN FRONT
OF THE PROSPECT
AND BUILDING RAPPORT

THE SALE PYRAMID

Get More Prospects

Sealing The Sale

Closing

The Sales Interview

Build Rapport, Qualify

Get in Front of the Prospect

Get a Prospect

You've got a prospect. Or a list of prospects. The second step in the pyramid is to get to them and sell something. That's your purpose — in a nutshell.

In what we're going to share here we'll be emphasizing one-on-one selling. We'll also be talking mainly about bigger-ticket selling. But everything will be useful in some way to everyone in sales. By studying the techniques I'm going to describe, you can actually increase your selling power at least tenfold.

I'm not ruling out changes or adaptations. Everyone in Face-to-Face Selling has to make adjustments and work out a face-to-face technique that's really comfortable. Or a telephone technique. Even in the same company no two people will go through a presentation in exactly the same way.

The key in "getting in front of the prospect" is the way you got the referral — and what you learned. Do you know about the prospect's personal situation, job, family status, and so on? Can you settle on a best time to visit? Is the prospect on shifts — a factory worker, perhaps, or a policeman?

The kind of information you need, and should get when taking a referral, depends on your product and the kind of sales effort you are making. You should know in advance what information will be most useful.

With people in business, you can sometimes offer — by phone — to visit early in the morning. Many sales people have used this approach very successfully. A number of business people have thanked me for visiting as early as 7 A.M. "You know what a hassle we have here during the day," they tell me.

When making the approach to the prospect, you will

want to control the conditions as much as possible. They needn't be ideal. But if you have a 10-, or 20-, or 40-minute presentation you'll want to be where you give the presentation — without interruption if possible.

Many Face-to-Face reps use the telephone. Once again, the basic rules apply. You have to project a pleasant personality. You'll want to try to control the conditions if you're arranging an interview. You'll still want to study this chapter carefully.

The Seven Steps

This chapter and the two that follow make up the core, the guts, of this book. The three chapters take you inside the Face-to-Face Selling process in three stages:

Chapter 6   Getting in Front of the Prospect — Building Rapport

Chapter 7   The Demonstration or Sales Interview

Chapter 8   Getting the Order

Those are the three chapter headings. But in these three chapters I'll be giving you a basic seven-step process, a tried-and-proven formula for success in selling. We have already talked about one of those steps — Prospecting. The other six steps fall in these three chapters like this:

Step 2: Getting in front of the prospect — included in Chapter 6.

Step 3: Building rapport and qualifying the prospect — also covered in Chapter 6.

Step 4: Showing the product or service — discussed in Chapter 7.

Step 5: The closing process — included in Chapter 8.

Step 6: Sealing the sale — covered in Chapter 8.

Step 7: Getting more prospects — discussed in

Chapter 8.

Self Awareness

Do you have to be aware of each step as you go through it? Not really. You have to be comfortable with what you're doing; you don't want to get too mechanical. But with practice I'm sure you'll find yourself realizing that you're on Step 3 or 4 or 5 and that it may be time to get on to the next one.

That has happened to me. Each demonstration seemed to flow more easily as I worked into my own system. The same will happen to you.

A Chapter 6 Thought

Character has been defined as the ability to carry out a resolution long after you're out of the mood.

— Author Unknown

I have to stress again that a lot will depend on the kind of product or service you're selling. The company you're working for will probably give you some carefully prepared guidance on what do to and what not to do. Or it may leave you entirely on your own.

Either way, you're going to find that all selling has elements in common. The techniques we're sharing here will be important to you **in some way.**

You're Unemployed If ...

Sales people who are serious about their work know one thing for sure. As a lot of direct sales companies tell their reps, "You're unemployed if you're not in front of a prospect!"

I agree totally with that philosophy. I've used it myself. So get out your prospect cards. From whom did I get this referral? Can you use the name of that person? Everything may be important.

Getting in Front

Some veteran sales people say that you could walk up to a house, ring the doorbell, and say "Good morning, Mrs. Johnson, there's an alligator out in the street" — **if** you have a smile on your face. And of course, as we have pointed out, a pleasant manner is critical. It's especially important in that first minute or so when you're trying to get inside the door.

Watch an experienced person do it. He walks up to the door, sets down his briefcase or kit or whatever, then rings the bell. When the door opens, he says, "Good evening, Mr. Doe, I'm Jim Morris, may I step in?"

I could be the salesperson in this scenario. The method has opened thousands of doors for me. I've set down my briefcase so that I don't look too formal or official. The prospect's eye wouldn't necessarily travel down to see the briefcase. I've kept the greeting as direct as possible.

Other sales people have techniques that differ slightly from mine. Mike Pankratz, a superb direct seller, prefers to say at the outset, "I'm wondering if you'd have a few minutes?" Others would use other wordings. Some would shuffle their feet on the doormat, as if cleaning them. That indicates that you're ready to enter and don't want to mess up the carpeting.

The really important thing is that you feel good inside

and show it. You show that you feel good about your work. As one author put it, you indicate that you don't need a checkup from the neck up.

Don't Try to Sell It on the Doorstep

You may, and very likely will, get a question from the prospect right away. The prospect may say, "What's it about?" Or: "Are you selling something?"

Answer No. 1: "I have a **few ideas** I want to share with you." Or: "I'm in the _____ field and would like to **share** some ideas with you." Or: "I was talking to Dorothy Jones and she suggested that I stop by."

Answer No. 2 (said with a smile): "Do I look like a salesman?"

The cardinal rule: unless your product absolutely dictates it, don't sell on the doorstep. That means you don't say, "I want to **demonstrate** something to you."

Ammunition in Reserve

You'll also want to have some ammunition in reserve. Answers to other possible questions. You don't want to get hung up on the doorstep.

One question our reps got frequently was, "Is it books?" My answer to that was usually, "It's more important than just books..."

With experience you'll learn to anticipate most of the possible questions. You'll develop your own answers that will open that door wider and get you inside. You'll work out statements like this that anticipate the no-time excuse: "Hi, I'm calling on busy people. May I —?"

Believability: The Magic Ingredient

From your first word you're trying to establish

believability. You can't — don't want to — say too much. You **do** want to listen. Even while talking your way in, you want to listen. As Christopher Morley says, "There's only one rule for being a good talker: be a good listener."

In a sense you're **listening** your way in — and making yourself believable at the same time. You're also learning about the prospect. You can gauge the family's economic status, perhaps see evidence of hobbies, check the location of the TV set, note the number of books, and so on.

You're talking just enough.

Keep It Noncommercial

If you are in selling, you say, you're **selling**. Then, how can you keep selling noncommercial?

By selecting the right words. Anyone can do this. At *World Book* a lot of reps used a statement like this:

"I was talking with Joanne Smith the other day. She saw and liked our **Program** and said I should meet with you to let you **evaluate** it too. I'm confident that you will find my **visit informative.**"

Notice the noncommercial words **program, evaluate, visit,** and **informative.** They pay the prospect a quiet compliment.

"Shall We Sit Here?"

You may not make it inside the front door. That happens at times to all Face-to-Face Sellers. In such cases I usually say, "Well, I'll call at a more convenient time." Sometimes I leave a packet of information.

If the prospect does invite me inside, the first thing I say is, "Shall we sit here?" My thinking is simple. If the prospect keeps you standing, you're not going to get

75

much of his time. But once everyone is seated, it's accepted
that something important and worthwhile is going to
happen. You have become a "guest." Many basic social
courtesies apply to both you and your "host" or "hosts."

Building Rapport

I mentioned the high school coach with whom I
worked one summer. He had what I'd call automatic
rapport with many of the families we visited. The same was
true of a school counselor who shared my work at a later
date. But the counselor's case proved that, once inside, you
have to make it clear that you have come to talk business.

The counselor knew everybody in town. After we had
been invited inside, it became a habit to chitchat for a
while. It made me very uncomfortable. Finally, before
making a call, I said to my "buddy":

"Could you open with something like this? 'Of course
you know me from school. I want to mention that I'm not
here on school business, though. I'm here to talk about
something that is quite important. I think it will be of real
interest to you'."

He agreed. It worked. We were covering our flanks. We
did not sneak up on people by whipping out a prospectus
after 20 minutes of gossiping. Some common sense is
required here. Calling on friends, you don't want simply to
drop in, visit for an hour, then spring your presentation on
them.

How about those thousands of other situations where
you don't have automatic rapport? Look at just a few ways
to build it...

● **Use the prospect's name.** And pronounce it
correctly. In a referral situation, you can usually get the

correct pronunciation from the person giving you the referral.

Many times I've had a prospect tell me enthusiastically that I had pronounced a name correctly. Often the prospect would add, "and few people do."

● **First name or last?** Opinion is divided. You certainly have to consider a number of factors before using a first name: age, position, the nature of the referral, and so on. You have to play it by ear. A fact: using first name builds rapport more quickly.

● **Comment on your relationship with the person who referred you.** "Your cousin, Bill Heath, and I went to college together" — that kind of thing if it's true.

● **Pay a sincere compliment or show sincere interest.** A compliment is praise that is deserved. Interest is attention paid to something that calls for it. You don't want to gush about something that doesn't deserve praise. But most people have at least some "conversation pieces" that you can refer to. People like to talk about such things.

As far as showing interest goes, the subjects are everywhere. Books. Skiing. Hobbies. Little Johnny's or Jennifer's progress in school. Regarding the last one, I made it a practice to say, "Are you satisfied with _____'s progress?" That would generally bring a thoughtful answer. I never said, "How is _____ doing in school?" That question seemed to hold a challenge.

In asking, "Are you satisfied...?" you generally get a more honest answer than you would otherwise.

Warning: don't get sidetracked for an extended period. Remember the counselor.

● **Talk of mutual friends or concerns, if any.** I'm amazed daily at how small the world is. Very frequently the prospect and I have found that we had mutual acquaintances. But I always made sure I left a positive image of the acquaintance.

It's my belief that you can find a common element linking you and the prospect in nearly all cases. It may be sports, religion, kids, cars — almost anything under the sun. But once you find it you will start discovering the power of mutuality. Both you and the prospect start feeling more comfortable. You've taken a big step toward a sale.

● **Use humor.** A little humor both relaxes the atmosphere and speeds up rapport building. Humor has to be in good taste at all times, of course.

Qualifying Your Prospect

You've been inside the premises two, four, six minutes? You should qualify your prospect quickly. "Qualify" here means you are finding out whether a sale is at least possible.

An outstanding sales person once told me, "I have only three presentations in me per day. Therefore I want to use those presentations on honest-to-goodness prospects."

That's sound thinking.

I've found that three basic questions have to be answered in the qualifying stage.

● Does the Prospect Have an Open Mind About My Product?

A prospect needn't be a "ready buyer" — someone who was looking for a place to buy your product or something like it. In most selling situations ready buyers aren't too plentiful. If they were, there wouldn't be any

78

need for a sales force. The company would be foolish to put out substantial compensation to salespeople.

I'm delighted when I bump into a ready buyer. But because there are so many who are not ready, I've always given priority to finding out whether the prospect has an open mind.

Some examples of the closed minds that sales persons have run into occur to me. A cosmetics salesperson found that the prospect had religious convictions prohibiting the use of cosmetics. In other fields, prospects may have used a product or service before and found it unsatisfactory.

● Am I Talking to a Decision Maker?

If you are talking to individuals, not companies, with experience you will develop skill in judging whether or not a prospect is capable of making the purchase alone.

We are living in an age of increasing independence for both spouses. Many wives make their own decisions to buy reference sets, household items, wines — and of course cosmetics. But if the wife is home and the husband away, and if she indicates that she and hubby do the grocery shopping together, you can bet that she probably won't make a buying decision alone — and that demonstrating your product to her alone is not a wise use of your time and energy!

● Can They Afford It?

Clearly, the size of the "package" you are selling can be a factor. So can family circumstances at a particular time. Heavy medical bills or a precarious job situation can convince prospects that this is not the time to buy. In such cases, it is possible that they can't.

Asking Good Questions The Right Way

Asking the right questions in the right way can be an important part of effective selling. Good questions are definitely needed in the qualifying process.

Good questions should do several things for you ...

— They should provide information that will tell you whether you're talking to the right person. This information should also help you determine what direction to take in the presentation.

Example 1: In selling books, do you stress in questions the pleasure or availability of the books for browsing or the very practical help they can give little Bobby? (The latter.)

Example 2: In selling a home, would you sell the potential for profit at resale or the pleasure it will be to live here? (The latter.)

Another Question Technique ...

In qualifying, you might use another question technique that has worked wonders for people selling financial products ...

"If I could introduce you to a program that has produced a 20 percent compounded return for the past decade, without a single down year, would you be interested?"

Questions and the Word What

With good reason the word **what** has been used very effectively in the sales process. The word doesn't put people on the defensive. It makes for brevity. And best of all, it can give you ammunition for the "how" — how you as the Face-to-Face Salesperson can help them.

Example: What is the biggest challenge in your current

sales operation?

Answer: Recruiting.

Salesperson: Very interesting. I'm really glad I came. I have a program that can do _____ for you.

Example: What is the most important thing you look for in shoes?

Answer: Fit.

Face-to-Face Salesperson: Great. That's our specialty.

Another big dividend: the prospect has just verbalized a need for your product or service.

It can work for you as it has for me. Take a moment, now, and think of a question of this kind that would relate to the product or service you sell. Write it down ...

"If I could show you a way ..._____

_____

_____ , you'd be interested, wouldn't you?

Any prospect who doesn't answer **YES** to a question like this is probably not going to be worth your while.

The ones who do answer **YES?** You've begun to condition them mentally to do something they haven't necessarily thought they were going to do.

Chapter 7

THE SALES INTERVIEW

I like to define selling as a process of negotiation. Both sides communicate — with gestures, signals of other kinds, pictures, symbols, words, written materials.

Communication, as everyone knows, has to be a two-way process to be really effective. In Face-to-Face Selling the two-way aspect may be more important than in any other kind of selling. The Face-to-Face Seller has to listen. Effective selling is not overpowering or trying to wear down the prospect. Salespeople who do those things may not only have nothing to listen **to;** they may lose sales. Or they may get **sales** and find cancellations waiting for them the following morning.

The direct salesperson has to have a prepared presentation. But that presentation needs to be flexible. **Every selling situation will be a little different.** The Face-to-Face person has to be ready to deal with those differences. **It's easier to speak forcefully if you know what you want to say.**

There are classic stories that show the results of memorizing a completely mechanical presentation. Two of them involve Face-to-Face sellers who memorized responses for given situations.

Case 1: Salesperson: Will your husband be home soon?
Wife: My husband is in the hospital.
Salesperson: Splendid! Now...
Case 2: Salesperson: What does your husband do?
Wife: He is deceased.
Salesperson: That must keep him very busy...

Creating a Need

The sales interview follows the approach to the prospect. In fact, the interview flows right out of the approach.

Your first challenge when you move into the interview phase is to build a need for your product. You may take only a few minutes to do it. But if you do it properly you increase greatly your chances of getting a sale.

In some cases the prospect will reveal a need without any prompting from you. A question may bring out the statement of need; or the prospect may "clue you in" with no hesitation.

Mentally Condition Your Prospect

More normally, you'll deliberately plant the need-seed. The material and method you use may come out of recent news. It may be statistics, facts, projections. The need you build should in all cases fit your industry, your product, your service.

Many sales companies provide their reps with sales tools that dramatize needs. If you have them, use them.

The 1984 report on education in the United States gave

every company selling educational materials for the home a perfect means of establishing a need.

As one expert *World Book*er told me, "I like to refer to that 'Nation at Risk' report. It makes the point that parents have to be concerned about their children's progress — at home as well as in school."

Can you think of a way to build a need that will fit your situation?

Inadequate, not Inferior

One of the most expert Face-to-Face persons I've ever met used to say that in building a need you were trying to make the prospect feel inadequate, not inferior.

I would describe the basic difference between those two words this way: **inadequate** would mean that the prospect feels that he or she has not done everything possible to correct a situation. But it's not too late to take corrective action (buy your product or service.)

Inferior would mean the prospect feels below standard in some way...permanently. The normal reaction would be anger or defensiveness.

Once again, the process of causing a prospect to feel inadequate depends more on how you say it than on what you say. But you do need relevant facts. You **should** come on politely. You **should** wind up with a question or questions to make clear the gravity of the situation is understood.

Obviously, "need" can flow from basic human motivators. Most of us want status or prestige. We also need acceptance, economic security, recognition, achievement.

Some topnotch sales persons see six basic reasons for buying: love, caution, fear, profit, utility, and emulation.

All those things help round out the picture. And give clues to needs.

Building and Finding

You can either **build** "need" or **find** it! Often, a simple question will bring an answer that uncovers a need.

Questions like these have worked for salespersons in various fields...

> "Are you satisfied with...?"
> "Are you interested in improving...?"
> "Have you a specific concern about...?"
> "Have you ever used our product (or service)?"
> "Do you know that cost studies show...?"
> "Do you think you have enough...?"

And of course don't forget what may be the best one: "If I can show you a way to..."

Painting Vivid Pictures

Need-building may be most effective if you can paint vivid pictures. That's true of the entire interview process, in fact.

Working recently with the salespeople for a pay TV service, I encouraged them to build needs by saying something like this to their prospects:

> "You work hard all day, Mr. Jones. In the evening, you deserve every bit of pleasure you can get out of your leisure hours. You've earned the right to

86

settle back in your favorite armchair with a cold one in your hand and share with your family the pleasure of watching a first-rate feature movie without a single commercial interruption. Haven't you?"

I don't remember any prospect saying, "No, I haven't." Over the years, I've sold thousands of sets of encyclopedias with the help of the following picture...

"Mrs. Smith, as your little Frankie goes through school, will his teachers see a bright, enthusiastic boy with his hand up, ready to answer...or will they see him with his head bowed, hoping not to be called on?"

Observe how some experienced salespersons selling financial products work. These Face-to-Face Sellers may encourage prospects to take steps to provide in advance for a youngster's college education...

"Bill and Mary, by setting up a program like this now, you'll have the peace of mind of knowing that the financial part of Julie's education is well taken care of. You'll be able to look forward to enjoying the same pleasure and pride that I saw in the eyes of some proud parents at the (college name) graduation ceremonies last spring. It's obviously a great feeling to be able to say to yourself, 'Yes, we've done our part in giving Julie the start in life we feel she deserves'."

Itemize and Summarize

I believe firmly in the power of itemizing and summarizing. You can carry a note-sheet in the breast pocket of your suitcoat. Or have notes on a pad. You can refer to them when you need them.

You may itemize several times in a presentation. Why not? It makes you look professional, organized.

In need-building a typical list of points might add up to a summary of the particular situation you are describing. For example...

"So you see, Mrs. Jones, what the situation is. I see three things here. One, the schools aren't capable of doing the job they would like to do. Two, that puts an extra burden on the parents. Three, without the kind of help that this program provides at home, a lot of youngsters have trouble in school.

"It's serious, isn't it?"

The Transition

You've built need. The prospect is thinking with you. Now you want to get into the core of your presentation.

You'll work out your own method of making that transition. It can be a few words, a few sentences. I've found this kind of thing very effective ...

"By the way, Mr. Martin, it doesn't matter what kind of job you're doing. I was raised in a rural area. I could see that a farmer couldn't do a very good job if he didn't have good equipment. If he had to go back to the sickle and scythe, he'd have a tough time feeding the nation — or even himself.

88

"You need equipment. The surgeon wouldn't do a very good job if he had to use Civil War methods. How would they carry out a heart bypass operation?"

"It's the same in the home. The quality of the educational situation at home depends on how good the tools are. That's why I'm here."

Transitions connect the steps in your presentation.

Showing the Materials

In addition to the product, your company may provide you with a sales talk, brochures, or other sales aids.

Be sure you use them to sell benefits, not features, as much as possible. Don't just show what the product is but what it will do for you.

Sell What the Prospect Wants to Buy

The real estate agent had a major passion in life. He believed houses should be engineered for efficient operation in all weathers.

The potential buyers had told him they were looking for style and living-space. The agent talked right past that expression of need. One home the couple looked at seemed to be ideal. But the agent buried them under BTU's, R values, and heat pumps.

Finally, the couple gave up. They left abruptly, leaving the agent scratching his head.

The agent was working from a sheet that gave a hundred details about the house. But he got "hung up" on those details. He forgot to be tuned in to what the prospects were telling him.

Worse, he sold features, not benefits, and certainly not style and space.

Using your materials carefully, you may give some parts of the presentation more emphasis than others. You have to use judgment there. You'll find that you're more comfortable with some parts.

But refer to all the parts at one time or another. If you're using fairly complicated material — a multilayered broadside, for example — you should comment at least briefly on each page or section that you show.

You want to keep it moving. Keep the prospect interested.

Selling Benefits

Harry Steinberg, a top Face-to-Face Seller, told me once that a price increase in his company's products wouldn't affect him at all.

"I sell benefits, not the pounds or the size or the color," Harry told me. "They could double the price. It wouldn't affect my sales at all. When you're selling a thousand dollars worth of what it will do for you, what's a 10 or 20 percent price increase?"

You're selling the mouth-watering sizzle.

Take a moment now to jot down the three most important benefits of your product or service.

Benefit No. 1:

_____

Benefit No. 2:

Benefit No. 3:

You may have the most impressive array of cosmetics on earth. Or of home beautifiers. Or of wines. Or of books. But the old sales training school adage is still true.

20 of the Most Common Objections

1. Can't afford it at this time.
2. We want to think about it.
3. I can't make this decision alone.
4. We may next year.
5. A relative or friend sells the same product.
6. You're coming at a bad time.
7. We have plans to spend the money elsewhere.
8. The price is too high.
9. It's recession time. We're cutting back.
10. We have no budget for your product.
11. Your company is too big (or small) to handle the order.
12. Your service wasn't good last time we bought from you.
13. We are satisfied with our present supplier.
14. I can't make up my mind.
15. You're too late; we've got one already.
16. Your product is old, out of date.
17. I don't like your company.
18. Your price sounds too low; I'm skeptical.
19. We've got one on order.
20. Your product hasn't been tested enough.

You may think an elephant is a beautiful animal. But that doesn't necessarily mean you want to own one.

Don't trust your product to sell itself.

The Lead Pencil

I'm not saying features are unimportant. They are. But the strength of that importance lies in translating each feature into a specific benefit — something the product **will do** for the prospect.

You could sell a lead pencil this way. Say the pencil has an eraser tip. You can simply tell the prospect that the pencil has lead in it and an eraser on the end. Those are the **features.**

What really interests the prospect is how those features translate into **benefits:** the lead is a highly versatile way to write or draw, and errors can be corrected quickly by erasing.

Handling Objections

"I ignore objections — politely," says one experienced Face-to-Face Seller.

Another: "I always have an answer ready. In fact, I've kept an objection file for years."

Those answers from two successful Face-to-Face persons show at least that different salespeople have different methods of handling excuses or objections. Depending on the objection and on the way it was said, my own response was either no response or something like this: I would turn the objection into a question.

"Then you really feel that ...?" I might add some facts that would counter the objection. I might ask more questions. But I am really trying to find out whether the prospect means what was said, and determine if that is the real reason he or she is hesitating.

In my experience objections very often have little or no direct connection to facts. Often, they are excuses. The prospect verbalizes them to take part in the sales negotiations. Or to defend himself. The prospect may be trying to slow down or halt the sales process briefly. Possible motives for doing so include the following:

● The prospect has not yet decided to buy.
● The prospect has other questions to ask.
● The prospect wants to let you, the salesperson, know that he or she is still "boss" — that you're not dealing with a pushover.

Remember that a sale is made in every presentation. Either you sell the prospect or the prospect sells you on the fact that it's impossible to buy at this time.

Objections are important in one way. They tell you what may be on the prospect's mind. They make Face-to-Face Selling a participative or two-way process. You should welcome them.

More on this in our next chapter.

Emotional Appeals

Regarding emotional appeals, you again find differing opinions. Some Face-to-Face Sellers are not comfortable using emotion, and avoid using it. Others use emotion very effectively!

Some things to remember about emotional appeals:

They have the purpose of leading the prospect toward buying, but if not made carefully and phrased right, they can have a reverse effect.

In one case, a salesperson facing the lady of the house was getting nowhere. An emotional appeal involving the man of the house seemed to be called for. The salesperson, looking at a picture of a handsome man on a mantle, said, "Is that your husband?" The response was affirmative. The salesperson went on, "He looks like a very nice man. I'm sure he always goes along with your decision." The answer came back at once.

"He's an S.O.B. — and I'm sorry I married him."

The salesperson said, "I guess I misjudged him." The salesperson's technique would have been effective in nine out of 10 cases. This just happened to be an unusual situation.

Common sense is necessary in using emotion in selling. You'll want to keep in mind that most prospects today are more sophisticated than they were 50, 25, or even 10 years ago. You'll want to respect their intelligence.

— The emotional appeal may be most appropriate in the "sealing the sale" phase (next chapter). In this phase you are trying to show your prospect-turned-customer that buying was a wise decision.

Making another Transition

Now you're moving into the Getting the Order part.

The transition many salespersons have found effective runs as follows.

"By the way, the nicest part about this is that it's so easy to have. (Take out the order pad.) Let me show you how this looks on paper...

Another method has worked wonders for me. It's actually just two simple points. When I've finished showing the product, I say:

"I really came here today to accomplish two things,

Mr. and Mrs. Johnson. One, I wanted to show you how you can benefit from having this educational program in your home. Two, if possible, I wanted to work out a way you can have it now."

You may at this point get a question on price. With bigger-ticket items, a lot of salespeople do one of two things.

● They do **not** say, "It costs three hundred and ninety-nine dollars." They do say, minimizing the figure, "It's only three ninety-nine."

● They do not mention the price at all. They write it on an order pad and show the figure to the prospect, saying...

"The good news is that, because of the volume of business we do, you can have it for this small amount."

"The salesperson watches for reactions, of course.

Both approaches work.

Chapter 8

GETTING THE ORDER

This final phase of the selling process seems to scare some salespeople, especially part-time salespersons. Some find it unnatural. They don't want to seem pushy or overbearing.

If you're feeling a little timid yourself, think of some facts. **You're not a professional visitor.** You're there on business, and the prospect knows you're on business. That means that at some point you're going to ask for the order.

Think of this, too, About 60 percent of all Face-to-Face Sellers **never** ask for the order, even one time!

The stance you take, the way you talk to people, the way you project — this is what Creative Confrontation is all about. You know that **How You Say It** is more important than **What You Say.** We've talked about hundreds of other things. But now we're at what may be the most important part of all.

Unless you ask for the order, you probably won't make the sale. You've wasted your time.

Remember what they say about Columbus. No one would have blamed him if he had turned back. But no one would have remembered him either. You need to persist.

The Closing Process
Some salespeople like to think of the conclusion or close of a sale as the statement of a few words, or a single sentence. That may be accurate where smaller-ticket items are involved. But I believe it's different with bigger-ticket products or services.

Here, it's a process. One that can be plotted step by step. One that anyone can understand and master.

As indicated earlier, the process has three basic parts: the closing process itself, sealing the sale, and getting referrals.

"Ask Early and Often"
An old sales rule holds that you should "Ask (for the order) early and often." The rule is a good one. But how often is often? One authority says four times. Another will tell you five or two.

My answer: it depends on your product or service. The higher the cost, generally, the larger the ticket and the longer your presentation and the more numerous your chances to ask for the order.

How often you ask may also depend on whether you are using the party plan or the one-on-one method. In party plan selling, orders may rain down on you. Or you will undoubtedly have a point in the program at which you ask for orders.

A kind of group psychology may take hold of those present. It may inhibit order placement or spur it on.

Usually it is wise to take the order **first** from the person who has the higher status in the group, providing it appears that person is enthusiastic about your product.

Kinds of Closes
Different authorities classify "closes" — the order-getting phase — in a variety of ways. You could surely find information on such formats as these ...

● **The Order-Pad Close.** You use your order pad as a selling tool. You may, depending on your style and what you're selling, have it in front of you from the moment you sit down. You personally fill out the order.

● **The Choice-Question Close.** I have found this one very successful. Again, you would use an order blank. But with it in plain view, you may want to condition the prospect a little more...

"If you felt this program was something that you were convinced would make a difference, I'm sure you'd be able to afford x dollars a week for it, right?"

The choice-question is appropriate now. To make it easy for the prospect, you'd say...

"People pay for it in one of three ways. Some pay cash. Some pay for it over 90 days, others use a monthly plan. Which of these three arrangements is most suitable for you?

If you get a positive answer, you would of course keep on writing. "What's the correct address here?" **Never ask the prospect,** "Do you want it or don't you?"
You see what's happening. You are giving a

something-or-something choice. You are not giving a something-or-nothing choice.

● **Impending Event Close.** You tie the close to something that may or will happen. The price of the product or service will be higher, for example.

A Chapter 8 Thought

Yesterday is a cancelled check; tomorrow is a promissory note; today is ready cash — use it.

Kay Lyons

● **The Additional Value Close.** In this case you reinforce the prospect's confidence in making a "buy-now" choice. You may repeat a story that makes a good point.

Other types of closes will occur to you. They all share one factor: you are asking for the order. Which one fits you best? You are attempting to "work out a way" for the prospect to benefit from your product **Now.**

With some prospects who still seem to be in doubt, you may be able to take stronger action. You reach for a phone and say, "I'm going to see if we can't get delivery in a week." With some prospects you can practically issue a direct order without offending them in any way.

"It's very clear that you want this program, I can tell. Go get your checkbook and we'll get the materials on the way to you."

The SATMC Method

You encounter an objection. You want to keep moving, but you have to deal with it. The old SATMC method I learned in my initial *World Book* training program may be your best option. The technique works in many different sales situations.

SATMC Stands for Five Words:

Smile
Agree
Turn
More
Close

The technique is simple. Hearing the objection, you **Smile.** You seem to understand, then you **Agree...**

"That's the reaction most people have, frankly." Now you **Turn** the objection...

"But you know, you mention that you can't afford it. I was calling on a widow lady the other day and she said, 'When I got this product, I had no business buying it. Financially I didn't. But I really felt at the time that it wasn't an expense, it was an investment. And there hasn't been a day in these past three years that one of the kids hasn't used it. I think it was the best money I ever spent.' "

So the excuse has been turned. But you're not done. You have to present **More...**

"By the way, I did neglect to show you one of the most beneficial things about this ..."

101

Now you move to **Close** again. But in a different way. You have choices and can invent hundreds of your own...

"I don't know whether your kids have ever received a package this size in the mail before. We could put their names on the box. Would that be okay or should we address it directly to you?"

Or:

"Does a member of your family have a birthday coming up? We could make this a birthday present."

Minimizing Cost

Minimizing the cost of your product or service gives you another way to close. In using this method you are making it easier for the prospect to buy. A common approach...

"You know, cost is pretty much how you look at things. Now, you know your situation and I don't. I'm on the outside looking in. But I do feel — well, I'm not going to twist your arm on this, but what does your grocery bill come to every week?"

"Okay, $100. Think with me about this. I'm sure you shop wisely to keep it at that. But what if you got your grocery bill once a year? Say the bill came in today and you had to tell your husband that it's $5,200. That would shake him a bit, right?"

"But you don't pay the grocery bill annually. You pay it weekly. Now, can you think of this product in those terms? You can buy it for $7 a week. Would it be a big deal if your grocery bill were $107 and not $100?"

Or:

"I was leafing through a college guide the other day. You could send your Peggy, if she were old enough, to X college for $6,700 a year. That's for nine months."

"At $6,700 a year you'd be paying more than $700 a month for tuition. That one month's tuition would be more than the entire price of this product. And the product might make the difference, perhaps provide that additional educational advantage to enable Peggy to go to that particular college."

You've made the cost look minimal. In a sense, of course, it is.

In most cases you can draw your comparisons on the basis of the prospect's income or business. For example, a substitute teacher might earn $60 a day...

"You're talking about one additional subbing day every two months to make the required monthly payment."

You Make the Decision

You keep moving as long as you're getting positive answers — or neutral answers that tell you you're on the right track. But — and this is vital — make the prospect's decisions as much as possible. You decide what the prospect needs.

Many inexperienced sales persons make one deadly mistake. They are showing several or many products. They have their literature out — then they ask, "Which ones do you like?"

In deciding for the prospect, you do it differently.

FACE TO FACE SELLING

Frequently, you can turn it to your advantage by
recommending that the prospect take only **Some** of
your items, or part of your package ...
"Some enthusiastic salespeople feel that everyone
should have everything. But honestly, your Bobby's in
fourth grade. He would benefit from these other
books, but — and I'm being very practical — I think
you need this one and that one. It'll cost you about
half as much."

An advertising space salesman — or any direct
salesperson — could do the same thing ... along these lines
...

"I believe, from what you've told me here, that I
understand your problem. In view of the message you
want to get out, I really do want to suggest that you
take a full page. And certainly in order to be able to
track the results of the ad, you need to run it a
Minimum of X number of times."

The Three-Point Close

Still meeting resistance? They want to **"think about
it"**? Try the three-point close. It brings us back to
enumeration, or itemization, that wonderfully handy tool.
It would go like this — with changes that adapt it to your
field ...

"I understand your point of view perfectly. I think
you **should** be discriminating about the buying
decisions you make these days. Let me suggest this.
Maybe I can think about it with you. I've been
counseling families for more than X years and frankly
I've found that the smart, discriminating buyers
generally do think about the same things.

"Number 1, they say, 'Is this the product I want? And I review with them. I say — and by the way, let me ask you — is there any question in your mind about the quality of the product? All right, that's one thing you look at.

"Number 2, smart buyers ask, 'Is this something that's going to be good for us?' I don't think I need to ask you about that, do I? You seem to feel as your neighbor Mrs. _____ did — that it's not an expense, it's an investment.

"Number 3 — and I'd be embarrassing you and insulting you if I suggested that you wouldn't answer yes to this. That's the third thing people ask themselves — 'Can I pay for it?' We have just discussed the three things most discriminating people consider when they 'think about it'."

"Let's go ahead and get the product on the way to you?"

"May I Be Candid?"

You have a terrific alternative to the three-pointer. Or, you can use this one **with** the three-pointer. It goes like this...

"Mr. and Mrs. Allen, could I be very frank with you — would I insult you if I were totally candid...?

"All right, I know you have good intentions on that, but I really do think that since Bobby has a reading problem you'll probably want to do something about it. It's better to do something now rather than later when you might have to spend a bundle on tutors. Or rather than take the chance that he'd have to live with the stigma of having to repeat a year in school, or do remedial work during the summer vacation."

The fact that you asked their permission to be totally straightforward allows you to be stronger with them without offending them with your candor!

Can you add a point here? Can you stress a service feature that's part of your package? I've found that it can really put a fine touch on your close...

"You know, you're not just buying a product here. You're getting my expertise with it because I'm as near as your telephone."

	Excuse	Meaning of Reply	(Testimonial, Objection	Follow-up etc.)	Close
Want to Keep a Closing File?					
Here's a Model Form					
Case 1.					
Case 2.					
Case 3.					

Those Vivid Pictures

Paint pictures — again. They can make getting the order so much easier. They may be more important in the order-getting part than in other parts of your presentation.

One that I've always liked goes like this...

"I notice you have rubber tires on the tractor out there. You say, maybe the kids will go through school without any additional help, and that may be. But I know 40, 50, or 60 years ago they didn't have inflatable rubber tires. You could probably still have a tractor without rubber tires, but certainly they give you a smoother ride through the fields, don't they?

"Now, I'll guarantee you that having these materials will give the boys a smoother ride through school."

Got a Sale? Stop!

Mark Twain tells the story of the man listening to the Sunday sermon. When the preacher started, the man was impressed. "I think I'll drop $10 on the plate," he thought.

The sermon went on. And on. "Maybe $5 will be enough," the man decided. A while later, with the congregation getting fidgety, the man thought: "This is out of hand. I'm not going to give a cent."

In the end the man **took** $5 off the collection plate.

The lesson for the Face-to-Face Salesperson is simple. When you've got a sale, **STOP!** You are not so wedded to your presentation that you have to run through it from beginning to end after you've made the sale. If you do, the prospect may react like the man in Twain's story.

Write it up. Seal the sale. And go.

Sealing the Sale

Morning dawns. The customer you sold last night has what salespeople call "buyer's remorse."

How bad a case is it? Will the customer call in and cancel? It may depend on how well you sealed the sale.

How Not To Sell A Radio

Author and sales trainer Al Robertson told how he once visited a factory to see a new product line. He learned **everything** about the product, a radio that could receive from a great distance. Since he had a store at the time he ordered some of the radios.

A customer came in, saw the radio, and asked about it. Al told him. The radio contained three miles of wire, had 746 soldered joints, and boasted a pre-amplifier tube and automatic sound control so that the sound would always remain at the same level. The details poured out.

The prospective customer became restless and nervous. Finally, breaking in during a pause, he said to Al: "Do you have one of these radios that you'd like to sell?"

"Yes, of course."

They completed the transaction. As Al rang up the sale, he asked what had motivated the customer to make the purchase.

"Not a thing that you said," came the answer. "In fact, if you hadn't stopped talking, I was going to leave. My brother-in-law told me that this was the only radio that would get Kansas City and I have a favorite program from there that I want to hear."

Tying the Package

Sealing the sale — or tying the package, as it's been called — means you are reassuring the customer. A lot of inexperienced salespeople neglect it, sometimes because the sale has put them on Cloud 9.

You are simply trying to make the customer feel good about the buy decision. You can do it in a dozen ways. But some that have worked for thousands of Face-to-Face Salespersons are these, spoken perhaps with a handshake...

"I want to congratulate you on having done something very important. You've taken a big step toward..."

And:

"You know, the nice thing about this is, the richest family here in Kenosha, Wisconsin, can't have a better
_____ because there isn't a better one."

And a really emotional one:

"When I see people like you investing in this product it reminds me of the college commencement I attended a couple of springs ago. A young man got up to give his talk and said, 'Ladies and gentlemen, before I start my talk I want to thank the person who's responsible for my being here today — my mother.' And some people there knew the circumstances. She was a widow, and had actually done menial work to put the boy through college. I thought the applause would bring down the rafters when she stood up. I noticed a lot of hankies coming out..."

"You know, this _____ won't solve all of life's problems, but it will certainly take you a long way toward..."

Believability — again.

Leaving Materials
You can seal the sale in other ways.

If your company makes them available, you can, for example, leave materials on the product or service. While waiting for the product to arrive or the service to start, your customers can be reading about it, learning about it.

If you don't have the materials, you have a reason for coming back. On the return visit, you may be able to prospect some more.

Getting More Prospects
Prospecting was the first of our seven steps. It's also the last. Getting referrals is a form of prospecting.

How many referrals do I try to get out of this last stage of the selling process? As many as possible. But I'll start by asking for two.

You can do it by offering a favor, not asking for one.

The Offered Favor
To me, it's just as simple, and more natural, if you believe in your product or service, to offer a favor. You can do it this way — or in any of many other ways...

"I've really enjoyed visiting with you. It's always pleasant to visit with someone who's as intensely intersted in _____ as you are.

110

"Has my visit been informative for you? You know, I don't have a lot of time, but you've been so nice, I'd like to take the time to call on two people in your circle who might benefit from seeing (this program, product, etc.). Who do you think would be the two most likely persons or families?

How One Firm Gets Referrals
Out of Seminars ...

Has This Seminar Been Informative?

Our goal is to make every seminar we conduct a very worthwhile experience for everyone who attends. We trust that it has been good for you.

You probably can think of several people who would benefit from attending one of our sessions. Would you take a minute and jot down their names? We will see that they get an invitation for a seminar in the near future.

Thank you for your help!

Name	Home Phone	Office Phone

Name	Home Phone	Office Phone

Name	Home Phone	Office Phone

Referred By: _____

At this point it may be useful to note that others are buying. The wealthy Van Husens down the street. A well-known pastor. A member of the city council.

If two names are forthcoming, I have primed the pump. But I don't stop. If the customer provides 10, I'm that much farther ahead. The endless chain.

Obtaining Information

You need to pay close attention all through this process. Make notes. Ask questions. A few more minutes may provide you with enough referrals to last a week.

You're actually trying to find out all you can about these potential prospects. If it's available, you need names, addresses, telephone numbers, work schedules — all the information we've talked about. You also need permission to mention the source of the referral:

"You don't mind if I use your name, do you?"

Every one of us is tempted to short-cut. We would like to show the product or sevice, or the literature on it, and say, "Listen, I've got something to show you." If you've resisted that temptation, and made your presentation, you can surely go the last mile.

That means: get referrals before you leave. Get them whether you made a sale or not.

35 Choice Questions or Closing Lines

1. Would you prefer to have delivery on a weekend or a weekday?

2. Would you like to use our monthly payment plan or would you like to pay cash?

3. I have just one of these discounted models (vacuum cleaner, set of books, etc.) left. Shall I reserve it for you?

4. We can add this additional product onto your order for 30 percent off the regular price. Shall we do this?

5. Would you prefer this in the blue or the red?

6. This product is a little higher, but I sense that you prefer quality. Would you prefer this one or the standard model?

7. Would you like to have it shipped in the children's names or your names?

8. These are probably the most comfortable shoes made. Would you like these or the ones with the higher fashion look?

9. You will be making an exceptional choice — this is a garment of exceptional quality. Shall we fit you for it?

10. Would you like to take it with you today, or shall I ship it to you?

11. We can guarantee this TV set for six months rather than the usual three. Is this important to you?

12. We can guarantee this price for four weeks if you order today. Shall we get it started?

13. This is the last week we can offer it at this amount before the price goes up. May I ship it to you now?

14. Shall we see how this painting looks on your living room wall?

15. This is a limited edition and we only have a few left. This may be your last chance to have one. Rather than risk not having it available, shall we order it for you today?

16. Would you like us to bill you the first of the month or on the 15th?

17. Would you feel better if we added credit life insurance to your order? Will this give you more peace of mind?

18. Would you like to take advantage of our three-for-the-price-of-two offer?

19. Don't you agree that this is the most attractive product of the entire selection?

20. Is this what you've decided on?

21. If you ever find a problem with the (any feature), just remember our "Quality Guarantee" and we'll replace it!

22. A person like yourself who appreciates quality should have this product. I'll work out a way that you can have it.

23. You save 25 percent by ordering the products as a group. Shall we do it this way?

24. I can hold it until tomorrow if you like — this product is selling quickly, and I want you to be able to take advantage of the order.

25. Why wait when you can enjoy the program (or other product) today?

26. I'd be insulting you if I suggested you couldn't afford x dollars a month, wouldn't I?

27. You can start with the basic program and order the other products within 90 days at the package price.

28. Would you like me to include the gift page for Bobby and Mary?

29. This product is really a superb investment as well as a good purchase with inflation being what it is.

30. If you order today, you can have x days to see if you are satisfied.

31. This is the same product that (a celebrity or respect person in the community) uses.

32. You're making a wise decision. This is the best (product) made in this price range.

33. Would you like to take advantage of the cash discount, or do you want to use your credit card?

34. For a person whose time is as valuable as yours is, I think you can see this is a good investment, can't you?

35. Will you be putting it in the living or the family room?

Chapter 9

SUMMING UP:
LEPRECHAUN PAT

Presentations. Attitude. Technique.

Their initials spell PAT. He's my leprechaun friend who holds the secret of success in selling. This book leads us naturally to him.

He gives me an opportunity to take apart this subject of Face-to-Face Selling in a slightly different way.

Presentations is easy to understand. It's that just-discussed, much-ignored process of getting in front of a prospect and giving your sales talk. In party-plan selling it involves getting in front of a group.

Attitude seems to me to be the sum total of all those personal factors we discussed in "You Are the Message." It makes you if you first shape it. Attitude carries you in rain or sleet, in high winds and snow.

Technique is the how. How do you go about selling? How do you present yourself? How do you give a presentation? How do you close? Improve your technique and you'll improve your results from the presentations you make.

Presentations
Manfred Esser came to the United States from Germany with an idea and a driving ambition. He knew no English, so he bought 15 German-English dictionaries. He placed the books in convenient places so he'd always have one to refer to.

In a few years Manfred Esser had built a party-plan wine company into more than a $25 million company. Using the party-plan technique, the company's Face-to-Face Salespeople sold — and sell — fine wines. Manfred now has his own company.

What is Esser's secret? "You have to put a lot of hours in. You have to work harder than the other guys. You have to get to the prospects.

"You have to 'make things happen'!"

Work, the Great Equalizer
Sounds like work? It is. Presentations are work and work is a great equalizer. It can make you the equal of company presidents, of captains of industry.

As someone said, the average person finds it easier to adjust to failure than to spend the time and effort adjusting to the sacrifices that lead to success.

Remember the lady whose son struck it rich? She found her sales work was fun. She refused to give it up for a life of ease.

118

Work, in Face-to-Face Sales terms, means presentations. But there's good news about presentations. If you'll just make enough of them, they get you the results — the income — you want. The house in the country too. The Cadillac. The family helicopter. You name it.

Obvious? Of course. But you'd be amazed if you knew how many Face-to-Face Sellers give up before they learn this simple point. They look around at others and decide they don't have some necessary assets that others have. They assume that means they're programmed to fail.

A Chapter 9 Thought

Prosperity is more than an economic condition;
it is a state of mind.

— Frederick Lewis Allen

Nonsense. We've seen that successful Face-to-Face people come in all shapes and sizes, from all kinds of backgrounds, from families large, medium-sized, and small.

Herbert Casson, a British writer, had another answer. As if to prove that anyone could learn to sell, Casson wrote:

"In the past ten generations you have had 1,024 ancestors. In the past twenty generations, you have had 1,048,576 ancestors. Therefore you needn't worry about what is 'born' in you. There's plenty of good and bad!"

Putting the Law of
Averages to Work

Yes, the Law of Averages can work for you. It does

119

that in this way.

When you go out to make presentations, remember that you're taking the Law of Averages along with you as a working companion. It will do a tremendous job of helping to make your work productive. Let me explain.

Suppose you go off to work and make a string of presentations. You find, after a while, that you're getting about one sale for every six presentations. That's a very useful piece of information. Now you know how many presentations you have to make to get the number of sales you need.

You also know that as long as you make those presentations, you will get those sales. Believe me, you will.

You may have to make three times as many presentations as the hotshot who picks up one sale for every two presentations. But if you have the energy and the motivation to work hard enough — to make enough presentations — you could end up with **more** sales than he makes.

That's the magic of the Law of Averages.

Write it Down!

We've talked about record keeping.

Now you can see another reason why it's so important. Unless you have a record of your work, you won't know what you Law of Averages is.

Keeping records may do something else for you. It may remind you that you've done shockingly little work in the past few days or weeks.

I've found that I have to do, every day, things that are directly related to generating business. The question always is: **on this particular day, have I sold someone, have I**

recruited someone to sell, or have I taught someone how to sell?

"I like this daily reminder because I carry it with me each day and it plays an important part in keeping me on track."

DO IT NOW

Day_____Date_____

I. IMPERATIVE

1. ☐ _____
2. ☐ _____
3. ☐ _____
4. ☐ _____
5. ☐ _____
6. ☐ _____
7. ☐ _____

II IMPORTANT

1. ☐ _____
2. ☐ _____
3. ☐ _____
4. ☐ _____
5. ☐ _____
6. ☐ _____
7. ☐ _____

121

Would you dare to carry a stopwatch on your selling calls to find out how much time you actually spend in front of prospects in a week or a month? You might be shocked.

How the Law Works...

You could graph it. You could show how the Law of Averages worked on 50 presentations made by a single Face-to-Face Sales person. You'd see, in one typical case from one selling field, that the average ratio of success was one in five.

But the presentations that work will never be one in every consecutive batch of five.

In a typical series of 50 presentations (see below), the first generated a sale. Then came a dry spell. In 12 presentations the salesperson garnered no successes at all. A lot of brand-new salespersons would quit at this point. They'd say, "I'm just not cut out for this business. Too many F's for Failures and not enough S's for Successes (or Sales)."

The Typical Record...

S F F F F F F F F F F F S F S S F S S F F F F F F F

S F F F F S F F F F F S F F F F F F S F F F

The more experienced salesperson hangs in there. He or she knows the Law of Averages will work its magic in time. In the above case, a streak of five sales was waiting in the next seven presentations. The inexperienced person

122

would have left just in time to miss the feast.

One way to look at the Law of Averages: remind yourself that, in a sense, you're "paying" for each win with a certain number of losses. If you average one in five, every four losses will entitle you to one win.

...And Works

And then, if you have a string of 12 failures, don't look at it as a disaster. Look forward with pleasure and anticipation to the three wins you've earned.

Because it will continue to work.

Some experienced, expert salespersons with a good product get that proportion of wins to losses down to one in two. That does NOT mean this salesperson sells every second prospect. It does mean that 40 sales will result from 80 presentations.

These are not hypothetical examples. They are reality. Both come from actual records. The first example dates back to an early point in my career, when I was getting 10 S's for every 50 presentations. At the time I was studying the techniques of some other salespeople who were getting one sale out of every two or three tries.

The second example — one in two — comes from five years later in my career. I had begun to pick up a little steam.

As I look back on my own progress in sales, I realize that I reached my targets because I made lots of presentations. Sounds simple? It is. It's as simple as the secret of the man who built a sales staff that sold $30 million-a-year worth of water purifiers. Asked what he teaches his salespeople about the technical point of the product or process, he says, "I tell them to say that the product works well and the water tastes good. "

From my own experience I've evolved one basic rule of thumb:

Before Going Home, Make One More Dem!
Successful salespersons in all fields use this approach. They may be ready to quit for the day and go home. But they have a few minutes left. They make one more call and record another sale.

Who Am I?
I am the foundation of all business. I am the fount of all prosperity. I am the parent of genius. I have laid the groundwork for every fortune...from [that of] the Rockefellers down.

I must be loved before I can bestow my greatest blessings and achieve my greatest ends. Loved, I make life purposeful and fruitful. I can do more to advance a youth than his own parents, be they ever so rich.

Fools hate me. Wise men love me. I am represented in every loaf of bread that comes from the oven, in every train that crosses the continent, in every newspaper that comes off the press. I am the mother of democracy. All progress springs from me. Who am I? What am I? I am Work.

— From Ohio Mason

Ed Benzing, an old friend, may be the perfect example of this spirit. He was managing and training salespeople in the San Antonio, Texas area. He signed all his sales bulletins with this Spanish touch:

"Juan Mor Dem. " One more demonstration.

In this way Ed reminded his salespeople that it always pays to make "one more dem. "

Think Quantity, Think Time

Nothing can be more important to your success than the sheer numbers of "people you tell your story to. " I don't mean to imply that the quality of your presentation isn't important. It is. The ratio of successful presentations to losses will certainly rise as you improve your attitude and your technique.

But real improvement may take some time and practice. Meanwhile, you can do a lot of selling just by doing a heck of a lot of presenting.

Presentations, to me, are like having a money machine in your basement. That machine may be capable of turning out authentic $100 bills. But it's useless until you turn it on.

Think time too. Beginners in Face-to-Face Selling have excused their relaxed approaches to presentations by saying that "the prospect will be there tomorrow. "

That may or may not be true. What is a fact is this: put off making presentations, or **one more demonstration,** and success in selling won't wait for you. It'll take off with someone else.

Remember that poem that spelled out what happens to those who wait?

Can't Afford
The bride, white of hair, stoops over her cane,
Her footsteps uncertain need guiding,
While down the church aisle,
With a wan toothless smile,
The groom in a wheelchair comes riding.
And who is this elderly couple thus wed?
You will find when you've closely explored it,
That here is that rare, most conservative pair,
Who waited till they could afford it.

Now Write it Down
Make presentations now, even deadly dull, boring ones.
You can count on getting sales.

I'm not recommending boring presentations, you
understand. I'm only saying that, if that's your present
style, you can count on getting some sales.

To make sure you follow through, write down in the
following spaces as many **action ideas** as you can think of
...ideas that you've generated during this discussion of
presentations. All of them should be ideas that you plan to
start putting to work immediately.

1. _____

2. _____

3. _____

Improving Your Law of Averages

You can get good results simply by making a lot of presentations. But, in the long run, it's easier to make more **effective** presentations. And that boils down to improving your technique.

One sure way to improve your technique is to **close** more often. Look at this example:

Number of sales required	5
Ratio of sales to presentations	1 in 5
Number of closes made per presentation	3
Total number of closes required to make five sales	75
Total number of presentations required	25

In the above, you'll have to make 25 presentations and a total of 75 attempts to close in order to get five sales. However, my own experience has shown me that, if you make more closes, you can reduce the number of presentations and still get the five sales. For example, if you increase the number of closes per presentation to five, you'll get the following picture:

Number of sales required	5
Ratio of sales to presentations	1 in 3
Number of closes per presentation	5
Total number of closes required to make five sales	75
Total number of presentations required	15

Result: **You've cut your presentations from 25 to 15 and you're still getting five sales!**

Attitude
We've got to talk now about A for Attitude. The second letter in the name of my leprechaun friend PAT.

Up to now, we've talked about how you can make all the sales you want just by making enough presentations. Once you're into the swing of that, your next chore is to start improving your attitude. Make them more effective and instead of getting one S — sale — for every five or six presentations you'll get one S for every three or four F's. Eventually you'll have one S for every two presentations.

Think of this thing called attitude.

Are You Hard to Sell?
The first and most important point that I want to make about attitude is this: if you're going to be good at selling, you have to be good at buying.

You don't have to squander the grocery money. But it's true that successful people don't "have to be sold on everything." They don't sit back with an air of skepticism and say, "Prove it." More often they say, "This idea worked for somebody and it can work for me. In fact, maybe I can make it work a little better."

Make Things Happen!
You may have seen this; I've seen it hundreds of times. Some experience in direct selling dramatically increases a person's "can do" attitude in other areas of life.

What change takes place? You begin to realize that if you concentrate on your **expectations of good things,** rather than worry about the possibly bad, you will make things happen the way you want them to.

Don't Kid Yourself About Your Presentations

As I've said, presentations are W-O-R-K. More than anything else, your success will depend on how many hours you spend in front of prospects.

Grab your trusty pencil again. And get ready to be ruthlessly honest with yourself. Check your answers to the following when you're quite sure no one is looking over your shoulder ...

1. So far this week, about how many hours have you spent in front of a prospect?

    2 - 5   6 - 10   11 - 15   16 or more

2. Last week?

    2 - 5   6 - 10   11 - 15   16 or more

3. What's your daily average?

    1 - 2   3 - 4   5 - 6   7 or more

4. On a typical day, how many "breaks" do you take for coffee, lunch, personal business, or just plain loafing?

    1 or 2   3 or 4   5 or 6   7 or more

5. How long is your average break?

    5 minutes 10 minutes 15 minutes 20 minutes or more

SUMMARY: On an average day, you spend _____ hours in front of prospects and _____ hours taking breaks.

You won't forever be asking, "WHAT IF something bad happens?" You will be saying, "I'm going to make something good happen."

As a ballplayer chasing a fly ball, you'd say, "If there's a way I can get to it, I'll catch it." Not: "What if I drop the ball?"

You Are What You Think You Are

What's your attitude toward yourself? That's the most important question you have to answer.

Pick up that pencil of yours again and jot down the following (be honest—no one's looking):

1. The three things I like MOST about myself are:

_____

_____

_____

_____

_____

_____

_____

_____

2. The three things I like LEAST about myself are:

_____

_____

_____

3. On a scale of 1 to 10, I rate myself:

1   2   3   4   5   6   7   8   9   10

4. On a scale of 1 to 10, other people would rate me:

1   2   3   4   5   6   7   8   9   10

Obviously, there are no right or wrong answers to any of the above. But doing this you can measure your own attitude toward yourself. **Then** you can give some thought to what you may want to change.

But remember again. We can change some things about ourselves. Other things we can't change. Know the difference and do what you can and should do.

Oddly enough, most of the time what we think of ourselves determines what other people think of us. Whatever that self-image happens to be becomes a message that we project to others. If your self-image is a good one, they will think a lot of you.

And vice versa.

Building on Strengths
Consider the stories of two Face-to-Face Sellers, Mary

and Rona. Mary was 62, Rona 23. Both were extremely successful.

Their attitudes impressed everyone who came into contact with them.

Both women worked in units that included salespersons whose ages ranged as far apart as those of Mary and Rona. But as their managers told it, their success boiled down to one very simple principle:

Build on your strengths and NEVER compare your weaknesses to others' strengths.

Let's think about this for a minute. At age 62, Mary could have compared herself to the 23-year-olds in her group. She could have said, "At 62 I'm too old for this game. I'll never be able to compete with those younger women. "

She said nothing of the kind. Instead, she took this attitude: "I'm 62. That means I've got years more accumulated wisdom than those young greenhorns. I'm bound to have more credibility with prospects than a kid who's wet behind the ears. "

And Rona? She could have said, "I just don't have the experience to make a success of this job. " But she didn't. She said, instead, "I'm only 23. I've got three times the energy of those older people. I know I can out-work them. I'll show 'em!"

The net result? Both were consistent winners. They built on their strengths.

You've Got Something Special

Thomas Jefferson once said, "I've never met a man who couldn't do **something** better than I can. " Coming from a man with an extraordinarily wide range of talents, that's a remarkable admission.

Jefferson recognized that **everyone** has something special going for him or her.

What are **your** strengths? Take a minute and note them down...

_____

_____

_____

Add an appendix if you need one. And next time you start feeling inferior to someone, just recall what you wrote above.

Now let's review what we've said here and in chapters 2 and 3 about attitude...

- Attitude is a very important part of success and can often overcome a lack of knowledge and extensive training.
- Avoid negative people like the plague. Their attitudes are horribly contagious.
- Cultivate positive, "Rainy Day" people.
- Set specific goals — but avoid the three pitfalls of goal setting. (If you can't remember them, go back to Chapter 3 and refresh your memory.)
- Plan a Life Agenda.
- Keep the luster in your daily living by reading or listening to inspirational materials.
- Self-image is your most important asset. Know your strengths and weaknesses, but NEVER compare your weaknesses to someone else's strengths.

Action Ideas

Action encourages action. On the lines below, or on a separate sheet of paper, write as many action ideas as you can think of—ideas that occurred to you during this discussion of attitude. These should be ideas that you plan to start using immediately.

_____

_____

_____

_____

Technique

Up to now, we've talked in this chapter about the importance of making lots of presentations, even lousy ones, to keep the Law of Averages working for you. We've talked, too, about how your attitude can help you make the most of every opportunity and in communicating a positive attitude to others.

Now I'd like to talk about the third letter in PAT's name — the letter T. It stands, as you know, for Technique. This is the one element in selling that offers you the most leverage for maximizing your performance.

Much of this book is about technique. But think of this:

In the area of technique you can set yourself the task of deliberately improving your Law of Averages ratio so that you get more sales with fewer presentations.

It's a Matter of How You Say It!

TECHNIQUE IS WORDS — SEMANTICS...

REMEMBER THESE...?

Say This...	Not This
1. **Your neighbors,** the Jones', are **proud owners** of our program.	**I sold** the Jones this program.
2. You will enjoy **evaluating** this program.	I'd like to **demonstrate** this product to you.
3. I have a couple of exciting **ideas** I'm anxious to **share** with you.	I'd like to **explain** some of the features of our product to you.
4. Here are some facts that you may find meaningful.	I'll be honest with you.
5. Does this explanation make sense?	Do you follow me?
6. For a total **investment** of	For a **cost** of
7. I'll need your OK right here.	Your **signature** is required here.
8. You have the **privilege** of carrying this as much as 30 months if you choose.	Your payments will run for 2½ years at this rate.
9. What sort of **deposit** would you like to put on this today?	How large a **down payment** would you like to make?

135

10. The best part of this is how easy it is to have. It is only this amount (point to amount on order pad).

The cost is only **four hundred** and ninety-nine **dollars.**

11. The **service charge** is only a **penny and a half per dollar** on the unpaid balance.

The **interest** is 1½% a month.

12. The session that you have an opportunity to attend is an **Evaluation Seminar;** an opportunity for you to **evaluate** [the product or opportunity].

I'd like you to come to our **sales training workshop.**

Once Again, Keep Track

You can't keep track this week and forget about it next week. Your records will be a shambles. You won't know whether you are improving from one in five or six to one in three or four — or whether you're improving at all.

Suppose you've passed through that hardest door of all to get through — your own. Assume you've done your homework. You have a prospect, you make a presentation. You chalk up a success.

Really chalk it up. Make a note, quickly, using whatever system you've adopted. Record keeping is another part of technique, one that enables you to say, "On such and such a day I was this much closer to my goals. "

The Steps Again

When I first started in sales, I heard a lot of terms.

Some seemed to be pure mumbo-jumbo. There were steps to the sale, for example, in particular the "Resolve to Buy" step.

I had trouble understanding some of those terms.

I know today that a few fundamental things should happen on the way to a sale. If you do these things, you'll Make Things Happen. There are seven of them. Here they are...

1. Getting a prospect
2. Getting in front of the prospect
3. Building rapport and qualifying the prospect
4. Showing the product or service
5. The closing process
6. Sealing the sale
7. Getting more prospects

Write them down. Carry them next to your list of achievements.

Improving the quality of your selling techniques will also help many of you to be better in a vitally important phase of your business: recruiting. Remember this:

Recruiting is a Pure Selling Job

Recruiting Salespeople

It's been said that "management at its best is a selling job. " Recruiting salespeople for Face-to-Face Sales is a "pure selling job" — pure and simple. The process is exactly the same:

1. Find a prospect (recruit)
2. Get in front of the prospect
3. Establish rapport
4. Give the interview (sell the merits of getting involved)
5. Close (have them make a decision)
6. Seal the sale

137

7. Get another prospect

Space does not allow for elaboration on this important topic (my next book will elaborate!), but here are a few quick tips on several of the seven parts of the selling process when specifically related to recruiting Face-to-Face Sellers:

● **Finding prospects** - The process is the same as in any other selling, but a reminder that PREJUDGING people and assuming they lack the "marvelous talent" you have to do the job is the biggest single mistake made in prospecting for recruits.

● **Interview** - Don't tell them what they will get from the business — tell them what you get from it! It's been my observation that AMWAY people have done a superb job of sharing their success stories with others. The AMWAY distributor isn't afraid to brag; that's smart. They understand that recruiting is a pure selling job.

● **Closing** - Don't ask them to make any tough decision; allow them to make a **no risk** decision — an opportunity to come to a training session. (You'll sell 'em there.)

Chapter 10

CONCLUSION — STRAIGHT TALK FROM BART

A topnotch salesperson was helping me get started. The sales interview seemed to flounder when the lady prospect told us she could not buy our product because she believed the world was going to come to an end shortly.

Her belief was based in religious teachings.

My mentor spoke softly, respectfully. "I respect your position," he said. "I make it a rule never to question anyone's religious, political, or other very personal beliefs.

"But what if you looked at it this way? What if you bought this product so that Johnny and Mary would have the use of it in the little time remaining to them? You seem convinced that they would enjoy having these books.

"And when the world comes to an end, you won't have to keep paying for them. "

That story illustrates the basic rule that Face-to-Face Selling has a logic to it, a common sense, a never-ending challenge. When you're getting into it, you may have growth pangs. But it's still enjoyable even when it's tough. It builds concentration and determination because — if you're like me — you have to force yourself at times to make that "one more dem. "

But that has been described as the common denominator of success: forcing yourself to do the things failures are not willing to do.

I made lucky choices of a son and a daughter. My daughter comes home with a teacher's comment that reads, "I've never seen such a positive young person. " My son, cast in the same mold, talks to me before the big baseball game. "How many hits will you get today?" I ask. "It depends on how many times I get to bat, " he answers.

It won't matter if either young person goes into Face-to-Face Selling. They will make their own decisions. But they are preparing for life in a way that I can appreciate. Maybe, reading the following random items that summarize my philosophy of selling, you'll find some nuggets that will help you prepare for bigger and better things in sales or life in general.

1. **The Power of Women in Sales.**

Sorry, fellas, I don't want to offend you, but I believe women are at least as good as men in Face-to-Face Selling and often better.

In my experience this has been the case. I'm not a psychologist; I don't know why. Women often seem to have the edge when it comes to being self-starters, being flexible, and having the desire to win. It just seems that the odds of a good woman salesperson making it big in Face-to-Face

Selling are often better than those of a man of equal talent.

A second point: there is really an exciting new world out there for the woman who may be in her 40s or a little older, who has been raising kids and probably doing a great job of it. Many times this woman has fantastic determination, drive, and initiative.

A Chapter 10 Thought

None of us ever have it made, the important thing is that we're **making** it.

Someone tried to explain this to me. After all, the theory went, a man has been out in the business world 20 to 25 years. He's 40 or 45, and just possibly may be burned out. At the least he may be very jaded. To the woman just getting started in selling at the same age, it's probably a whole new ballgame!

The bottom line: you're making a terrible mistake if you assume that women aren't every bit as good as men for sales positions.

2. Age and Late Bloomers.

Some companies launch management development programs with the very definite suggestion (which I'm not sure would even be legal) that no one over 40 years of age should be accepted. I think this is a ridiculous strategy. I've seen so many incredibly good people who entered the selling field for the first time in their 40s, 50s, or even 60s!

There have been many good examples of this. Colonel Sanders, the founder of Kentucky Fried Chicken, is one of the best. He was 65 when he started his tremendous business.

The highest producing personal seller that I ever recruited was Harry Connor from Wilmington, Delaware. At age 57, Harry entered the selling field, after retiring from the ministry. He was truly an incredible seller for the next decade.

More recently, while attending the Harvard Advanced Management Program, I had a classmate who was preparing for one of the six general manager spots in the huge Barclay Bank organization. Interestingly, Trevor held only very low ranking positions in the bank for many years.

Then, something happened. Trevor decided to advance. He earned 11 promotions in seven years, to my mind a truly remarkable accomplishment.

I see enough examples similar to Trevor's to lead me to believe that people can blossom at almost any point in their careers. The late bloomers are very prevalent throughout the world in many different endeavors.

3. **Prep School and/or Ivy League Background.**

In many types of business organizations, the particular college or prep school you went to, or the connections you have, can have a very great impact on whether you get that first job. A lot of my attorney friends tell me the name and prestige of their law schools were important factors in their career successes.

In most Face-to-Face Selling opportunities, your school background and social status don't have a major impact on your upward mobility. The reason is because you simply have to perform every day. You have to make it happen. I've always believed, too, that you can get a good education at Podunk U. and, possibly, as much as I admire the school, an average one at Harvard.

If you have a strong work ethic, the chances are you've got a leg up in the selling field. I have not seen too many big successes in direct selling who came from wealthy families, but I've had very good results with people who are hungry and who have had more than their share of struggles in life.

I hope none of this turns off those lucky ones who were born to wealth.

4. Weather.

One of my major turnoffs is the nightly television newscast on the weather. It turns me off because there's not a single thing you can do about the weather. I'm going to try to feel good whether it's snowing or raining, or whether the sun is shining. Since there's nothing I can do about it, I intend to put in a good day's work and have a productive, worthwhile day regardless of what the weather is.

I will make this positive. If it's raining, I am reminded that people are likely to be at home. If there's a snowstorm, I am going to "see my neighbor." In short, I will see some of the good people in the community in which I live, people I probably have neglected for the past six months or six years. By having an umbrella and a raincoat in my car I'm always ready for the rainy day.

5. Sweating the Small Stuff.

A dangerous habit: I continually see salespeople who are negatively affected by the fact that they have lost an order to someone. They'll sit around losing five more while stewing over the fact that they should have had a

143

commission that they missed — or that someone stole an organizational order from them. Before they know it, their attitudes have cost them 20 organizational orders. We have to be very careful that we don't get into snits over insignificant matters.

I could give you a whole catalogue of examples of this. So, if we want to make big things happen, we have to be very careful that we don't sweat the small stuff.

6. **Training.**

We need to remind ourselves that it takes real character **to ask for** training. I've pointed out in another part of the book that you shouldn't worry about what you don't know. That's true, but all of us need training. And there are a variety of ways to get it.

Someone said once, "How long should you train a person?" The answer was, "How long do you want him to be good?"

Look for the good points, as noted earlier: the strengths that people have in the training area. Make notes, think about it, brush up, rub elbows with the person who is performing. I place a high premium on training.

As a matter of fact, even if there were a commission difference between two companies, given the choice I would join the one that appears to have a good solid training program.

7. **Commission Business.**

Recently I read an article that said if a company is simply offering only commission as compensation, and not a salary, that's a "red flag" — don't join that company because reputable, respectable companies just don't give people commission opportunities exclusively; they pay salaries.

I personally think that's a lot of baloney. I know a lot of very fine companies that offer incredible opportunities — and don't pay salaries. They do, in fact, put it in on the line and say, "Look, you'll be paid what you're worth. "

I like the commission business because it allows me to earn exactly what I'm worth based on my sales results. When you are paid only on salary, remember that your salary is overhead and a liability to your company.

When you're on commission, you're in a profit-generation situation. In effect, the income you get is in proportion to the profit your sales generate. How important is this? Very important. It gives you tremendous job security. Organizations that pay people on a commission basis are unlikely to be laying people off when the market gets a little soft. And their market probably isn't going to be as soft because their salespeople are going to be out **Making Things Happen!**

During the four major recessions we have had in the past 15 years, the direct selling organizations I've been associated with have had unusual selling records. The key salespeople in these organizations actually increased their personal selling results during the recession periods. This doesn't mean that it was easier to sell (I don't believe that it was easier). But I'm sure that everyone worked a little harder.

8. **Several Selling Jobs at the Same Time.**

With very rare exceptions, if you have more than one sales position at a time you are costing yourself money.

Frequently, we see examples of professional athletes with multi-million dollar contracts who aren't able to give peak performances, because they are distracted by "too many brief cases". If an individual is earning mega-bucks in one profession it just isn't smart to dabble in other things which can be a distraction. Most folks can only concentrate on one thing at a time.

9. **Opportunity for Promotion.**

Many salespeople worry whether there's going to be an opening for them when they are ready for a promotion. It's been my observation in more than 20 years in selling that it's very rare that there won't be a promotion available for a person who is ready for it!

If you're interested in upward mobility, and are in the selling game, prepare yourself — be a performer — get the job done, and when you're ready the odds are very much in your favor that the job will be ready for you.

10. **Prestige of the Selling Profession.**

Even today, a lot of people in this country do not understand the importance and the professionalism of the selling business. At the risk of offending people with public service organizations and with civil service-type jobs, I've observed that some of these individuals sometimes turn up their noses at people who are in Face-to-Face Selling, particularly direct selling.

The fellow who hired me into direct selling had the right attitude. I asked him about prestige — because I was a school teacher. I was an **educator,** as they say down South. He sneered and said, "Prestige among whom? The people who count will realize that you have a heck of a lot more prestige and that you're doing something more important when you're making things happen in sales than if you were teaching." He pointed out that I would be able to influence more people in a positive way as a successful salesperson than as a teacher.

I've always taken that attitude. But, unfortunately,

146

some people don't understand the selling business and fail to comprehend how vital selling is to a free society. They don't know that it's not mass production that made America great — it was mass merchandising!

If you feel good about what you are doing, and you are taking home the big paycheck, and you are growing personally, that should give you all the prestige you need.

11. How About the Car You Drive?

Very early in my career I was happy to be driving a relatively big car. School principals occasionally saw my shiny new car and said, "Gee, you must be making a lot of money on the books you sell. " My comment was, "We don't make much on them, but we sell a lot of them. "

As long as it's neat and clean, I doubt if the car you drive has any significant impact on the business you get.

A former boss of mine summed up my philosophy on the car question. He said some salespeople feel the price of the car they drive will determine their effectiveness in attracting other salespeople. He said that he probably wouldn't want to hire a person who made his decision on a career opportunity on the basis of the kind of car a person drove.

12. Boredom.

This country has a problem today. I saw a statistic recently that showed that 80 percent of all American workers are bored stiff. The article said that assembly line workers have 52 weekends a year and five days of drudgery in between.

That's one of the great benefits of the selling game. If you are a person interested in growth, in making things happen, in learning your job, you will never suffer from boredom in Face-to-Face Selling.

147

13. Sickness.

"I don't feel good. I need a day off. " Familiar words?

I've been blessed with good health. As a matter of fact, I haven't been sick in bed a day in 25 years. I have been very fortunate.

It is understandable that anyone can occasionally need a sick day for a heavy cold, the flu, or some other malady. But I believe there is a lot of truth to the statement, "I don't have time to be sick!"

I simply believe that a person who takes 10 to 12 sick days a year has a problem. I've never seen a dynamic leader or a big performer in selling who has taken those 10 or 12 days on a regular basis. Feeling good, to a great extent, is a state of mind.

14. Physical Fitness.

I'm not going to climb on a soapbox and talk about religion, politics, or physical fitness. With regard to fitness, however, I happen to believe that staying reasonably fit is an important asset if you're going to be a pacesetter in the selling field. Most sales jobs are pretty physical and require energy.

You need — everyone needs — to have a program that suits you to stay physically fit. Whether it's walking, the exercise bike, jogging, swimming, whatever. Aerobic-type exercises may be best. There is definitely a high payoff on the time that you spend keeping physically fit. Some people say, "I just don't have time to have an exercise program. " An excuse?

I personally find that with 30 or 40 minutes a day with a good exercise program, I need at least an hour's less sleep. So the "time excuse" doesn't stand up. Get in shape. It has a high payoff.

15. Changing Jobs or Companies.

I subscribe to the notion that the rolling stone doesn't gather much moss. Generally, it seems, people who change jobs because they had personal problems with the boss are, in fact, taking those problems with them.

Remember, there is a learning curve on most jobs. If you're going to get ahead, and want to be very good at your job, you need to spend some time at it. However, I will acknowledge that it is possible to get into a job situation where change is advisable. Examples: the unstable financial condition of a company, or the discovery that the company's product is no longer competitive.

An intolerable management situation also can develop. Or you may find yourself in a dead-end position. But, in most cases, incredible opportunity is right in our own backyard, or maybe in the position you are in right now.

16. Financial Stability.

A rule of thumb: spend a little less than you make. The big problem is that salespeople adjust too quickly to increases in their incomes. They make X amount of dollars a week, then double their income to $1,000 per week for a few weeks. They've been living on half of the new figure, but immediately adjust to a $50,000 lifestyle, based on commissions for a short time.

This can be dangerous. Better to pay yourself a salary and put a little money in the bank. Early in my career, I was motivated toward having financial stability because I observed that many of the veteran salespeople I was working with didn't have two nickels to rub together. Many had been selling for 25 years and more.

What to do? Many things. Example: take 10 percent out of your earnings each week and invest it in a blue-chip investment. If you're young, you're bound to be wealthy by the time you're ready to retire.

17. Handling Success.

How do you handle success in Face-to-Face Selling? It's a legitimate concern. Some persons get cocky. Some turn into conspicuous consumers. Or, even worse, they stop doing the things that made them successful.

This can happen when a salesperson receives a substantial promotion. Moving up the management ladder in the direct selling organization, I found that it was easier to be the best each time I got promoted because usually many of the people at my new level had stopped doing the things that enabled them to get the job. If they hadn't stopped doing them, they were usually not doing as many of them.

I don't subscribe to the Peter Principle. I don't believe that people usually get promoted to positions they can't handle. I believe people generally are capable of doing the job if they are really committed to doing it. They become incompetent only when they decide they've "arrived." Work, especially the amount of work that got them there, is no longer necessary.

CLOSE

In case you are peeking at the back of the book before you've read it, I'll tell you what you are going to get from reading it — or if you have already read it, I'll remind you of what I've said.

● **Get as Big a Slice of Life as You Can Get** — this is not a trial run, this is the real thing! When the opportunity arises, **GO FOR IT!** Reach for the Stars, and you may not reach a Star, but you won't come up with a

150

handful of mud.

● **Confront Creatively** — Being the best that you can be means that you need to confront each opportunity you have every day. Creative confrontation means "facing things boldly". It means coming to grips with each of life's challenges, rather than just hoping that problems will go away. This means reminding ourselves that — *EVERYTHING IS A SELLING JOB.* (I mean this in a totally positive and wholesome way.) The sales process explained in the book works. Use it!

● **Deliver All That You Promise!** — The growth companies, and the star salespeople of the late 1980's and 1990's are going to be those organizations and individuals who are service oriented — those who do a little more for the customer than they have to do. Whoever said, "Help enough others get what they want, and you will get everything you want" was right on the button.

Appendix A

Model Record-Keeping Files

Monthly Goal System

Monthly goal setting depends on a total plan of action involving a specific amount of activity on a daily basis. The amount of activity will vary according to various factors such as closing average, average commission per sale, etc.

	Minimum Quota	Goal
1. Total Income Needed		
2. Total Sales Needed		
3. Average Commissions Per Sale		
4. Law of Average		
5. Total Presentations Needed		
6. Income Per Presentation		

Record of Weekly Activities

Week Beginning _____

Program for Problems

It is important to remember that my activity program should be adequate to allow me to reach my sales goals in spite of unexpected problems.

Weekly Goals						

Actual Activity

	Attempts to Get in Front of Prospect						
	In Person	Phone	Presen.	Sales	Referrals	Earnings	Other
Monday							
Tuesday							
Wednesd-ay							
Thursday							
Friday							
Saturday							
Total							

After each day's activity, I should be proud to **write it down!**

Place this in a prominent place on or above your desk!

Weekly Goals

1 _____	19 _____	37 _____
2 _____	20 _____	38 _____
3 _____	21 _____	39 _____
4 _____	22 _____	40 _____
5 _____	23 _____	41 _____
6 _____	24 _____	42 _____
7 _____	25 _____	43 _____
8 _____	26 _____	44 _____
9 _____	27 _____	45 _____
10 _____	28 _____	46 _____
11 _____	29 _____	47 _____
12 _____	30 _____	48 _____
13 _____	31 _____	49 _____
14 _____	32 _____	50 _____
15 _____	33 _____	51 _____
16 _____	34 _____	52 _____
17 _____	35 _____	
18 _____	36 _____	

Keep your goals and your progress in front of yourself all the time! A handy record like the one below will accomplish this!

For Pocket Calendar

Month	Goal	Results	+ or −
Jan			
Feb			
Mar			
Apr			
May			
Jun			
Jul			
Aug			
Sep			
Oct			
Nov			
Dec			

Appendix B

Principles of Effective Phone Work and

a Sample Telephone Presentation

10 Basic Points for Successful Phone Work

1. Your purpose is usually to introduce yourself, or get an appointment — not to sell. The selling will be done at the appointment. (In some cases, you may be selling the prospect on attending a free workshop or seminar.)
2. Sell the prospect on what the appointment, evaluation session, etc. will do for them. Sell benefits — sell benefits — *sell benefits!*
3. Convey a sincere, friendly, and helpful attitude on every call, both by your tone and your content. Your mental attitude is the most important factor in successful telephoning.
4. Be optimistic. Think success. Show conviction. Be proud of your job and your company.
5. Repeat your prospect's name often.
6. Be tactful in your choice of words, particularly when asking questions.
7. Take the lead in the conversation and keep it. If the prospect takes charge, your chances of getting the prospect to do what you want are greatly reduced.
8. Be alert. Listen to the prospect's reaction to your offer as it progresses. Then capitalize on any sudden or unexpected response.
9. Learn when you are ''wasting your time'' with a prospect and politely end the conversation.
10. End the conversation once the offer or invitation has been accepted.

After each call, you should not forget to take the following step immediately:

1. Record the results of your call and any follow-up that is required.

Telephone Prospecting

Telephone prospecting should be conducted at hours convenient to prospects and appropriate to your business.

Good evening Mr./Ms. _____. My name is _____ and I'm calling for (company). Our company is sponsoring a free seminar on tax-reduction strategies for individuals and families. The seminar will be held at the Marriott O'Hare on June 20 beginning at 7:00 PM. I would be delighted to mail you a personal invitation if you would like to be our guest.

This is a sample of telephone talk used by a firm with which I was associated, for the purpose of getting people to attend a free seminar.

Answer to Negative Response

Mr./Ms. _____, the seminar is purely informative; you will not be asked to purchase anything at this seminar. The purpose of this seminar is to introduce our company to you and to show you how the service we perform can help you to assure your own personal financial success. The only investment we ask you to make is that of your time, which you will find to be one of the best investments you will ever make. I would be happy to send you an invitation.

Positive Response

Fine, I'm sure that you will find this seminar to be highly informative and helpful. Will you be bringing anyone with you? (List number of people.) Thank you. We are looking forward to meeting you at the seminar.

Telephone Confirmation

This confirmation should be used a day or two before the seminar.

Good evening, Mr./Ms. _____. My name is _____ from _____. I'm calling to make sure that you received your invitation to the seminar that our company is sponsoring (time/date/location.) Mr./Ms. _____, I believe you indicated that you would be (bringing a friend with you), (coming alone), (bringing your spouse with you), is that correct? (Confirm.) Mr./Ms. _____, we'll be looking forward to meeting you.

Appendix C

Suggested Telephone Talk

Telephone Talk for Making a Selling Appointment

"Hello, may I please speak to _____? (Wait for a reply.) "_____, my name is _____ and (Sue Smith) gave me your name. How are you today?"

At this point it is very important that you wait for a reply. (You will get one.) The goal of this presentation is to keep it as conversational as possible. If you remember this at all times and don't rush, you will get great results! If you can hear that this is a busy time for her, say:

"Can I take a minute, _____, or is this a busy time for you?" (Wait for a reply. If the time is not good, suggest that you will call her later that day, or ask if tomorrow would be better. Be brief! No one wants you to take precious minutes away when she is harried anyway. You then call back at the suggested time.)

If she gives you permission, proceed as follows:

"I was visiting with (Sue) the other day to show her some special materials designed to help prepare her (Bobby) for school and she thought that you too might like to know what is available. She thought I should give you a call. I would like very much to meet you and explain this (program) to you. Do you have a little time this week that we can talk about it together?" (Wait for a reply...The first thing to do is to *suggest a day and time;* if that is not convenient, suggest another. You may ask if she wants her husband to see this as well, in order to determine if it is to be an evening appointment.) After you make the appointment, ask if it is necessary to check with her the day before. If she says no, then say you will look forward to meeting her next _____.

There is always the possibility that she will forget the appointment. If she lives far, or if you want to check the night before rather than take the chance of an unfulfilled call, when you check, *Don't ask if the appointment is*

164

still on! Say instead that you are calling to verify her address:

"Is the number 47 or 49? I couldn't read my handwriting." In other words, *assume* you still have the appointment and are calling to verify some other information.

If the parent you are calling on has older children, rather than saying that you called on (Sue) to show her material to prepare her children, etc., you can say:

"I was visiting with (Sue) the other day to show her about it and thought that you might like some information about it as well. She suggested that I give you a call. I would very much like to...," and proceed to ask for a convenient time for an appointment.

The purpose of a referral call is to *Get the appointment.* It is not a good idea to go into a sales presentation on the phone *unless she asks you direct questions.* Even under these circumstances, give out only enough to whet the appetite. You want to visit in person when you will have an advantage.

If the prospect seems nervous about committing herself to an appointment but you feel there *is* some interest there, suggest mailing information. Generally a review/reprint is a good idea, followed by a call to see if she received it and had any further questions about it.

Remember, *each call* will bring you closer to a sale. Relax; don't rush it and, above all, be flexible about your responses. This is not the *only* prospect you will get. The next call will bring you *wonderfully exciting things* — interesting contacts, money, a whole host of possibilities.